D0266393

BLACK
GOLD

EDITED BY Ian Robertson

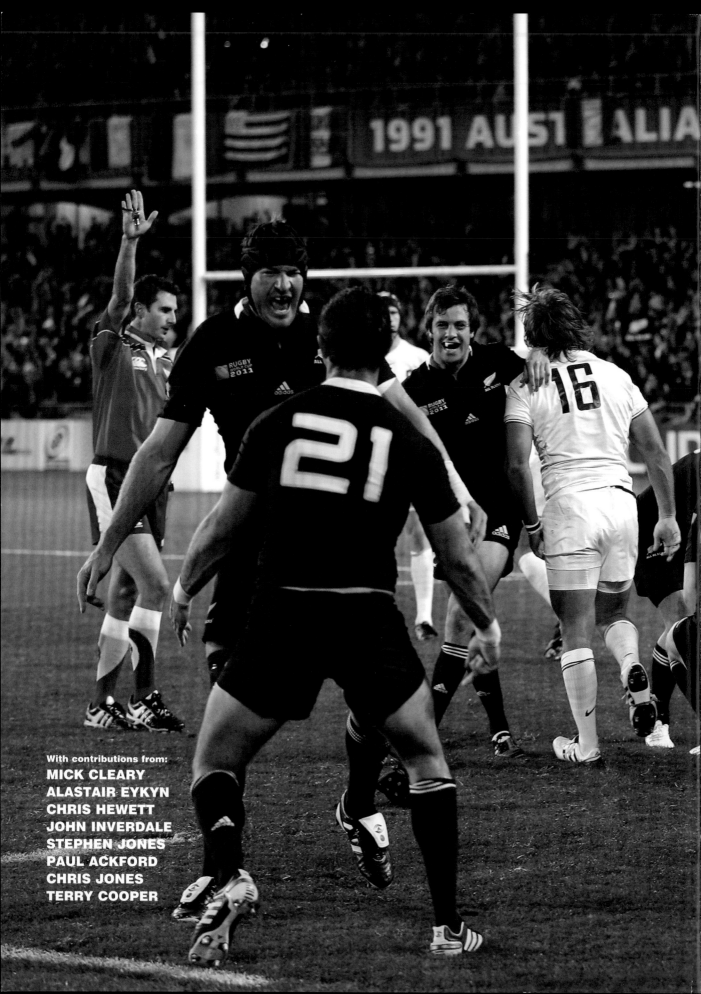

With contributions from:
MICK CLEARY
ALASTAIR EYKYN
CHRIS HEWETT
JOHN INVERDALE
STEPHEN JONES
PAUL ACKFORD
CHRIS JONES
TERRY COOPER

RUGBY
WORLD
CUP
2011

BLACK
GOLD

EDITED BY **Ian Robertson**

G2 entertainment

This book has been produced for G2 Entertainment Ltd
by Lennard Books
a division of Lennard Associates Ltd
Windmill Cottage
Mackerye End
Harpenden
Herts AL5 5DR

This edition first published in the UK in 2011
by G2 Entertainment Ltd
PO Box 11067,
Chelmsford, Essex CM1 9RY

ISBN 978 1 908461 30 8

Production Editor: Chris Marshall
Design Consultant: Paul Cooper

Printed and bound by
Butler Tanner & Dennis, Frome

The publishers would like to thank Getty Images for providing
all the illustrations for this book and would also like to acknowledge
the contribution of all their photographers:
Dave Rogers, Shaun Botterill, Alex Livesey, Warren Little
Stu Forster, Cameron Spencer, Sandra Mu, Ryan Pierse, Phil Walter, Mike
Hewitt, Martin Hunter, Hannah Johnston, Hagen Hopkins, Mark Kolbe, Teaukura
Moetaua, Steve Haag and Duif du Toit of Gallo Images and Paul Ellis, Greg
Wood, Gabriel Bouys, William West, Philippe Lopez, Martin Bureau, Franck Fife,
Marty Melville, Stephane de Sakutin, Christophe Simon and Peter Parks from the
Getty Images/AFP team

CONTENTS

5 star service
from Scottish Life

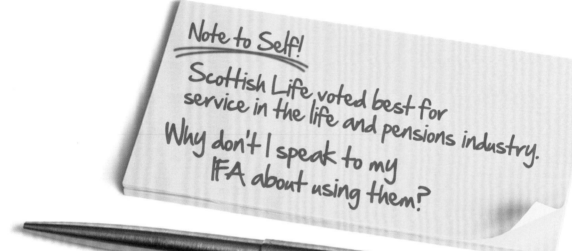

More and more people are coming to Scottish Life for their pension – we're ranked number 1 for service in the industry and can offer you the reassurance that comes with being part of Royal London, the UK's largest mutual life and pensions company. And as a mutual, we're not driven by shareholder's short-term demands instead we take a long term view of what's best for you.

For more information about Scottish Life speak to your financial adviser or visit www.scottishlife.co.uk/number1service

FOREWORD

Scottish Life is very proud to be the main sponsor of this book, which provides a fantastic account of the 2011 Rugby World Cup.

This seventh Rugby World Cup has proven once again, that the tournament is a magnificent shop window for the game of rugby union. We have been reminded of the rivalry of the southern and northern hemispheres and of the continuing rise of the quality and competitiveness of the so called 'second-tier nations'.

In previous tournaments some star players have emerged, but in this World Cup it's been very much about the teams. The eventual winners were the New Zealand All Blacks who hosted the tournament and won the competition for the first time in 24 years in a gripping final against France. Although no-one will forget the contribution of the courageous Welsh side.

Rugby perhaps foremost among team sports shows us the value of determination, team spirit, hard work and self-belief.

I hope that once again this book will provide rugby fans with a lasting and vivid keepsake of a memorable tournament.

John Deane
CHIEF EXECUTIVE
SCOTTISH LIFE

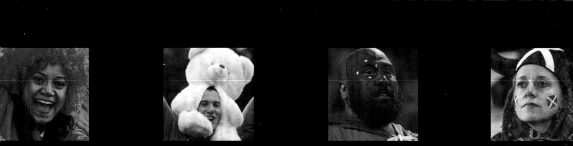

RUGBY WORLD CUP 2011

THE TEAMS

INTRODUCTION
ONE GREAT VENUE
CHRIS HEWETT

AStadium of Four Million? That's a big stadium by anyone's reckoning, yet the New Zealanders behind the 2011 World Cup production – principally Martin Snedden, a Test-class pace bowler for the Black Caps in his sporting pomp and now the man charged with delivering on the pledges made to the tournament's custodians during the bid process – always believed the men and women of the silver-ferned nation would throw themselves heart and soul into the competition, just as their Australian neighbours had eight years previously.

What could not be foreseen was the unforeseeable, at home and abroad. The economic downturn sparked by the 2008 banking implosion and accompanying credit crunch was bad news, both for those travelling from Europe and for New Zealanders anticipating a surge in business. As for the earthquakes that struck the South Island city of Christchurch, one of the major centres of World Cup activity, in the year leading into the tournament, here was a thoroughgoing

tragedy. Suddenly, Snedden and his colleagues were confronting the most profoundly challenging crisis ever faced by organisers of a major sporting event – not least because so many of those trying to bring the tournament to fruition were personally affected by nature's assault on the great rugby province of Canterbury. As Snedden wrote in an email to this correspondent after inspecting the serious structural damage to the recently refurbished Lancaster Park venue, 'It's a bloody sad day. New Zealand is a small place and the degrees of separation are tiny. We all have family or friends caught up in this.'

Within weeks, Christchurch was declared off-limits. The place where Richie McCaw and Daniel Carter, those modern-day titans of the All Black team, play their rugby – the city that has spawned almost 80 internationals, from Bob Deans of the 1905 New Zealand 'Originals' to top-ranking players like the centre Ian MacRae and the flanker Alex Wyllie – would not play an active role in the biggest sporting event ever staged

Fireworks set the Auckland sky alight as RWC 2011 is opened on the evening of 9 September.

in the country. A number of teams promised to pay the stricken town a visit, including England, who would have been based there had the original schedule held, but it was scant consolation for the local sporting community. To have made such a contribution to a country's rugby life and then have to step back and watch the ultimate celebration of it unfold everywhere else … Snedden had it right. This was indeed 'bloody sad'.

Yet in the face of all this, the organisers were still able to piece together a fixture programme taking in towns and cities across the land, all of which had one thing in common: a deep, century-long attachment and commitment to the sport. The Test venues of Auckland, Wellington and Dunedin absorbed the matches that would have been played in

Christchurch, while smaller hotbeds of rugby passion, from Whangarei in the far north of the North Island to Invercargill in the far south of the South Island, from New Plymouth and Nelson in the country's western reaches to Napier and Rotorua in the east, put their own unique spin on the preparations. No other country on earth could do it quite in this way, for here were 12 Gloucesters and Llanellis, a dozen Limericks and Toulouses.

Where did it begin, this great coming together of rugby nations? In the purely competitive sense, it was in one of the more unlikely parts of the world; that is to say, the Caribbean, where, in the third week of April 2008, the Cayman Islands played Trinidad and Tobago on Grand Cayman in the first match of the qualifying tournament. (For the record, the

visitors won rather handsomely, 39-12, and continued winning until they ran into Brazil.) In reality, however, the seeds were sown on a cold winter's day in Dublin two and a half years previously. It was there that the council members of the International Rugby Board (IRB) decided that New Zealand, rather than South Africa or Japan, should be awarded host status for 2011.

To say the very least, this decision was not universally acclaimed. Many commentators believed the Springbok nation to be best placed in terms of tournament delivery. For one thing, they had staged a brilliant World Cup in 1995; for another, they would be able to use new facilities constructed for the football version, which would be going ahead in 2010.

ABOVE Players train in Dunedin's Otago Stadium, the first venue in the world to have a natural grass playing surface under a fixed roof. **FACING PAGE** England manager Martin Johnson views some of the extensive earthquake damage inflicted on Lancaster Park (AMI Stadium), Christchurch.

Others believed the time was right for Japan, one of the so-called 'emerging' nations that seemed to have been emerging for ever and a day, to demonstrate that the union code could break free of its traditional confines and announce itself as a sport with global potential. A competition in All Black country would, they thought, be both a conservative choice and a sentimental one – a notion that gathered momentum when the leaders of the New Zealand campaign openly admitted that the country would never again be strong enough in economic terms to bid for the rights.

It was a close-run thing. Had South Africa, eliminated after the first round of voting, made it into the second and decisive round, there is no guarantee the New Zealanders would have prevailed. But prevail they did, and from that point they fired every best shot they could find in their armoury. The IRB, committed to a £150 million investment in rugby development programmes and heavily dependent on the World Cup to underpin that level of spending, accepted the financial reality of their decision, openly acknowledging that the yield from this tournament would be way short of

that from the 2007 competition in France. But with England, the sport's commercial powerhouse, due to host the tournament in 2015, this was not entirely calamitous.

So it was that the New Zealanders set about a major construction programme: a new stadium in Dunedin to replace rickety old Carisbrook, equipped with a transparent

BELOW Tourism New Zealand's Giant Rugby Ball exhibition centre set up for business at Circular Quay, Sydney, in September 2010. **FACING PAGE** London, December 2008. Martin Snedden, CEO of Rugby New Zealand 2011, after the completion of the pool draw for RWC 2011. The qualifying process for the tournament was still in progress when the draw was made.

POOL A	POOL B	POOL C	POOL D
New Zealand	Argentina	Australia	South Africa
France	England	Ireland	Wales
Tonga	Scotla...	Italy	Fiji
Americas 1	Europe...	Europe 2	Oceania 1
Asia 1	Play-off W...	Americas 2	Africa 1

roof made of ethylene tetrafluoroethylene (obviously) and blessed with an audience acoustic guaranteed to have the hairs on the neck pointing upwards; a redeveloped Eden Park showcase venue in Auckland; and significant improvements everywhere else. They also launched a multi-million dollar promotional campaign, based primarily on a mobile exhibition centre in the shape of a giant rugby ball. This appeared in some of the world's most striking locations: in front of the Eiffel Tower in Paris and Tower Bridge in London, at the Tokyo Tower in Japan and on Circular Quay in Sydney.

The financial outlay, lavish by New Zealand standards, was considered to have been worthwhile, but in truth most appetites were whetted the moment the pool draw became clear. In Pool A, the All Blacks would find themselves sharing the same rectangle of grass as the French, their conquerors in both 1999 and 2007, while Argentina, whose podium finish last time out was one of the great sports stories of the decade, were bracketed in Pool B with both England and Scotland, not to mention the fast-improving Georgians. From the English perspective, this looked like the easiest

group to win, while at the same time being the easiest group to mess up.

Pool C was equally intriguing. Australia would start the competition as top seeds, with Ireland, so successful in Europe at both club and international level since their calamitous campaign in 2007, as the second-rankers in this group. The unfathomable element? Italy, slowly ascending the performance ladder thanks to their regular exposure to Six Nations rugby, the intelligent leadership of Nick Mallett and the concentration of home-grown talent into two regional sides. But it was Pool D that really caught the eye, to the extent that experienced World Cup watchers described it as the strongest, least forgiving group in the tournament's history.

South Africa, Wales, Fiji, Samoa – what a quartet. You had to feel for the Namibians, who found a way past Tunisia to claim the one available qualifying place awarded to the Africa region, only to land with an almighty splat in the

World Cup's version of the 'group of death'. If anyone felt worse than Jacques Burger and his brethren from down Windhoek way, it was the Welsh. As if being drawn with the reigning champions was not enough, they would have to confront two South Seas teams in the uncomfortable knowledge that Pacific Island rugby had never been to their liking. Samoa had knocked them out of the 1991 tournament and beaten them again in 1999; Fiji had done for them in an exhilarating match in 2007.

At least Wales could draw on some hardened New Zealand know-how now that Warren Gatland, a long-serving hooker who played second fiddle to Sean Fitzpatrick for his entire All Black career, was running the Red Dragon show. He would not be the only silver-ferned coach working in an offshore capacity: Robbie Deans had taken charge of Australia; John Kirwan, a World Cup winner at the inaugural 1987 tournament, would return to his homeland as head man of Japan; Kieran Crowley, a former Test full back, was performing a similer role with Canada; Steve McDowall, who had once joined Kirwan in laying hands on the Webb Ellis Cup, had agreed to knock the Romanian scrum into shape.

Nor would the competition be short of Wallaby input: Brian Smith, a veteran of the 1987 competition, was with England; Toutai Kefu, a champion No. 8 in 1999, was with Tonga; Kefu's fellow forward from that vintage, the hooker Michael Foley, was with Fiji; John Muggleton, who masterminded the supremely effective Australian defensive operation in that tournament, was with Georgia. Many of the best tactical and strategic thinkers in the sport were heading for the Antipodes determined to make this World Cup more competitive than any of its predecessors. The feeling before kick-off on New Zealand v Tonga night in Auckland was that

they had every chance of succeeding. Particularly after the Tongan team, armed with players born in New Zealand, arrived at the airport in Auckland and spent three hours, rather than the customary 25 minutes, making the road trip into town. Thousands of expat Tongans thronged the streets to greet their countrymen – singers, dancers, autograph-hunters, well-wishers. Five days before the start, the Stadium of Four Million was beginning to fill up.

BELOW Kick-off approaches. The opening ceremony is in full swing at Eden Park ahead of the New Zealand v Tonga curtain raiser. **FACING PAGE** In 2007 Argentina shocked France by beating them (17-12) in the opening game of their own World Cup and went on delivering surprises to finish third in the tournament, beating France again in the third-place play-off. Was there a side in RWC 2011 waiting in the wings to emulate Argentina's deeds of 2007?

SOME ARE
MADE OF MORE

GUINNESS

ESTD 1759

GUINNESS

POOL A
BLACKS CRUISE THROUGH
PAUL ACKFORD

The Tongans were ecstatic. Six thousand of them had turned up at Auckland airport to greet their team, delaying the arrival press conference by hours.

Down by the waterfront the excitement was contagious, as cosmopolitan groups of supporters gathered amidst the flamethrowers and the stilt-walkers, before heading up along the two-hour fan trail walk from downtown Auckland to Eden Park. Tonga against the All Blacks, the first fixture, a riot of colour, comment and potential. The 2011 Rugby World Cup was up and running.

Not for long. On the tournament's opening night the headlines were more about Auckland's transport meltdown than New Zealand's relentless first-half display in which they piled on 29 points against a strangely lacklustre Tongan team. The stadium announcer advised those at the ground not to return to the cordoned-off area around the harbour. 'It's full,' he said. 'You won't get in.' New Zealand peaking too early? It seemed that way, as on the pitch the All Blacks throttled back, allowing Tonga into the match and prompting questions over whether this New Zealand team had the killer instincts of generations before. One game in and already the pressure was building on these All Blacks.

Elsewhere in Auckland, across the bridge at North Harbour, the gaze was on France, New Zealand's nemesis in 1999 and 2007, who were beginning their campaign against a Japanese side coached by John Kirwan, one of the All Blacks' great wingers. What kind of France would we see? That was the question New Zealand wanted answered, and, for an hour at least, it was fractured France; turned off, moody, diffident France – as Japan, playing with tempo and accuracy, got to within four points of them at 25-21.

Japan's outside half James Arlidge was the guy pulling the strings. Not the most authentic-sounding Japanese name,

■ Left wing Richard Kahui touches down in spectacular style for one of New Zealand's 13 tries against Japan in Hamilton.

but that's because he wasn't. Arlidge, born in Hamilton, New Zealand, kicked off his professional career with the Auckland Blues and the Highlanders before leaving for pastures new. Kirwan and Arlidge, two New Zealanders underpinning a Japan campaign. It felt a touch strange. Then Morgan Parra and the French locks Pascal Papé and Lionel Nallet weighed in with a try each inside the last quarter to restore a semblance of propriety to the scoreboard, and some familiarity to national consciousness and identity.

Two hours north of Auckland, on the road to the Bay of Islands, Canada were waiting in Whangarei to get their first Pool A fixture under way. Whangarei was waiting too. One of the more enlightened moves from the organisers of this World Cup was to shunt the smaller teams to smaller venues. Whangarei's spanking-new Northland Events Centre stadium was jam-packed for Canada's encounter with Tonga, and packed to the rafters for Japan against Tonga later in the pool. Whangarei had launched a campaign. 'Paint the town red', it was called, on the basis that the three teams to feature in that part of New Zealand all wore red shirts. If that sounds corny, it wasn't. Locals were encouraged to support one of Japan, Canada or Tonga alongside, of course, New Zealand.

▬ RIGHT The scrum disintegrates with the ball emerging for Japan as the Brave Blossoms keep the French in check until the final quarter. ABOVE Caught by the Tongan defence, Sonny Bill Williams gives a trademark offload to Richard Kahui in support. FACING PAGE, TOP Short on killer instinct? The All Blacks still racked up six tries against Tonga, this one by Jerome Kaino (centre).

LEFT Fly half James Arlidge, who plies his trade with Nottingham in the RFU Championship, scored all 21 of Japan's points against France. FACING PAGE Pat Riordan and bearded flanker Adam Kleeberger get to grips with Sione Timani as Canada beat Tonga 25-20. BELOW The moment of glory for Canada as the final whistle sounds in Whangarei.

The endorsement was heartfelt, the atmosphere, when game time came around, electric.

But something was still up with the Tongans. For the second time they failed to turn up and a minor upset was delivered. Driven on by the biblically bearded flanker Adam Kleeberger, Canada came back from seven points down with 16 minutes to go to beat Tonga 25-20, after another beardie, lock Jebb Sinclair, had scored Canada's first try. Back home in Canada a 'Fear the Beard' campaign was launched. Facial hair became a motif for the pool as, later in the competition, some of the militant French side grew, or bought, moustaches in a show of solidarity with Dave Ellis, their defence coach.

Whangarei wasn't done. At the end of a week which saw New Zealand despatch Japan 83-7 and France cruise past

POOL A BLACKS CRUISE THROUGH

Canada 46-19, Whangarei hosted its second and final fixture, involving Tonga and Japan. There was much at stake. Tonga were seeking to halt a run of five defeats by Japan, and Japan were after confirmation that they could be competitive when they got to host their own World Cup in 2019. There was something else on the game too. Old-fashioned national values. Two days before the match, Kirwan took his team to a forest to sit silently under a kauri tree called Tane Mahuta,

the King of the Forest. At 1500 years old, Tane Mahuta is New Zealand's most venerable tree. It stands almost 52 metres tall and has a girth approaching 14 metres. Kirwan quoted a Maori proverb. 'To have hope and faith in the future, you must first stand on the shoulders of the past,' he said. It was the present that vexed Kirwan and his team, though. Tonga beat Japan 31-18 in a match covered by 40 Japanese newspaper reporters and an additional 20 photographers.

Back in Auckland, fear stalked the streets as the All Blacks' decisive pool match with France loomed. It couldn't happen again, could it? An All Black campaign derailed by an out-of-sorts French outfit surfing on a tide of emotion. That was the narrative in 2007. In the conference room of New Zealand's team hotel, Dan Carter, the understated magician at outside half and the repository of a nation's prayers, revealed he hadn't reflected on that 2007 quarter-final. The comment was met with incredulity. 'Seriously, Dan? You haven't thought about that game at all? Because a lot of us think about it every day,' said a Kiwi hack.

The foreboding was everywhere. In the papers, on television, in the bars and cafes around Auckland's Queens Wharf, the social hub of the World Cup. 'What do you think, mate?' a morning television presenter asked a chef as he knocked up his dish of the day, a scallop and bacon combination. The response was long and informed, the minutiae of the recipe drowned in the whirlpool of yet more rugby chat.

Boy, was it intense! 'Did you need counselling after 2007?' Carter was asked. 'No. I was pretty good. I shot away and went travelling for a couple of months, and by the time I got back I was over it and ready to move on.' That was Carter's kingdom, a prison of expectation and recrimination. Jerome Kaino, a flanker who lined up alongside Richie McCaw, fielded a question ahead of the match. 'How honoured are you to be part of McCaw's 100th cap?' Kaino went into overdrive: 'It's huge for me. It's pretty special. He's obviously an exceptional player and done a lot for the game. He's someone I've respected and looked up to and learnt a lot from. It's a real honour for me.'

██████ **FACING PAGE** Tongan wing Fetu'u Vainikolo leaves lock Toshizumi Kitagawa of Japan flailing in vain at Whangarei's Northland Events Centre. **BELOW** Master finisher Vincent Clerc grabs another score for France against Canada in Napier. The right wing finished with a hat-trick in Les Bleus' 46-19 win.

New Zealand needn't have worried. France were good for all of ten minutes before the All Blacks, with Carter magnificent, cut loose to score three quick, match-eviscerating tries. A star was born along the way. Not Sonny Bill Williams, he of the chiselled body and risky offloads, but Israel Dagg, a full back so quick, decisive and enlightened that he was preventing the veteran Mils Muliaina from collecting his 100th cap. McCaw got his that night. It was presented by Jock Hobbs, the former All Black flanker and the administrator credited with bringing the World Cup to New Zealand, and the ceremony brought a tear to the eye. Hobbs is suffering from leukaemia, and the effort it took for him to get to the pitch for the presentation and the gratitude from McCaw that he had done so were heart-wrenching.

With New Zealand safely through to the knockout stages as top dogs, attention turned to France against Tonga. There was talk of civil unrest. French coach Marc Lièvremont had ditched François Trinh-Duc, his first-choice outside half going into the tournament, replacing him with Morgan Parra, a scrum half by choice and experience. Lièvremont was said to have lost the respect of his team, and was described by one observer as 'a father in the morning and a mother in the

RIGHT 'Quick, decisive and enlightened', All Black full back Israel Dagg torments France as New Zealand lay the ghosts of 1999 and 2007. **BELOW** Soane Tonga'uiha and co. scatter Frenchmen in their path as they drive upfield in Wellington. **FACING PAGE, BELOW** The Tongan squad celebrate their historic 19-14 win over France.

afternoon', a reference to his dishing out extraordinary public rebukes to certain players and then following them up with private love-ins hours later. Thierry Dusautoir, the captain, cut a lonely figure, downcast, isolated. Dissent filled the air. It was not good.

The match was a disaster for France. Tonga, stoked from the start by their inspirational hooker Aleki Lutui and fired during the match by scrum half Taniela Moa, ripped into the French. The inequality was staggering, a country with a population of 104,000 up against one with 62 million. But Goliath trembled and faded as Tonga kept up the heat. They built a half-time lead of 13-6 and held on as France came back at them with a late try. The final scoreline of 19-14 sent shock waves reverberating through the tournament, but it was the manner of the victory which was as impressive as the result. The last few minutes involved a pumped Lutui taunting the French front row at scrum time. France's humiliation was complete, yet even with two defeats in their four matches they found themselves in the quarter-finals because they had picked up three bonus points compared with Tonga's one.

Still the drama of the pool was not over. On the day before New Zealand's final match with Canada in Wellington, pictures of a stricken Carter lying prone on the ground, his face etched with pain, began to appear on websites around the world. A nation held its breath, but no relief was forthcoming as All Black doctor Deb Robinson confirmed the worst fears. On the fourth kick of the captain's run, a light training session 24 hours ahead of the match, Carter had torn his left adductor longus tendon and would play no further part in the tournament.

▬ **Moment of heartbreak. Dan Carter, New Zealand's nonpareil playmaker and goal-kicker, limps off the training field past worried team-mates, and out of the 2011 World Cup.**

2011

Alisi Tupuailai of Japan is held by All Black Sam Whitelock in Hamilton.

POOL A
BLACKS CRUISE THROUGH

What they said...

New Zealand: Graham Henry (coach) on Dan Carter's injury

▤ *It is a tragic situation for a highly talented young sportsman. This was his [Dan Carter's] scene – a World Cup in New Zealand was going to be his big occasion. He is certainly one of the great All Blacks.*

New Zealand: Dan Carter (fly half)

▤ *The night after the injury was pretty tough. I may be calm. It was different behind closed doors.*

New Zealand: Steve Hansen (assistant coach) to Colin Slade, Carter's replacement

▤ *Be Colin, not Dan.*

France: Marc Lièvremont (coach)

▤ *After losing to Tonga I thought I had experienced everything in terms of shame. But this time, it's an extremely violent feeling. Each missed pass, each missed tackle, I took as a deep personal failure. I would have liked us to gather around a few drinks, to talk, to share thoughts, to tell each other that it's a beautiful adventure. And I was disappointed. I got us some beers. Then we split in different directions.*
For now, there is no divide in the group, even if it may look like it. I've got respect for them. I think it is reciprocal.

France: Julien Bonnaire (flanker) on losing to Tonga

▤ *I don't think we can do any worse. We survived and that's the most important thing.*

Tonga: Andrew Ma'ilei (centre) on beating France

▤ *We built confidence from the Japan game. We were going to play physical up front for the first 20 minutes and then see if we could carry on. We did.*

Tonga: Kisi Pulu (prop)

▤ *We were confident that we could upset one of the biggest teams in the world.*

Tonga: Siale Piutau (centre/wing)

▤ *There's a lack of resources, but we're happy that with the exposure from this win we could get some help from companies and maybe the IRB. It's a massive day for Tonga.*

Tonga's Suka Hufanga holds off Julien Bonnaire to score.

Canada: Kieran Crowley (coach)

▤ *We did not achieve our objectives in the New Zealand defeat, but after the first three games I was pretty happy. The Union came to me some months ago and asked if I'd sign on again, because they didn't want World Cup results to affect their decision. Thank God that happened before losing to New Zealand. I'll be there for another 18 months.*

Japan: John Kirwan (coach)

▤ *We wanted to show the world how much Japanese rugby has grown. The world has stood up and said we play a fantastic style. Rugby at our second tier is a journey. What you see is only the tip of the iceberg.*

OFFICIAL WATCH OF
RUGBY WORLD CUP 2011

1860 Edouard Heuer founded his workshop in the Swiss Jura.

1916 First mechanical stopwatch accurate to 1/100th of a second.

1969 First automatic chronograph.

2011 TAG Heuer CARRERA Calibre 16 Day-Date.

Available at TAG Heuer boutiques and selected fine jewellers nationwide.
For more information visit www.tagheuer.com

RUGBY
WORLD CUP
2011
iRB
TOURNAMENT SUPPLIER

TAGHeuer
SWISS AVANT-GARDE SINCE 1860

POOL B
ENGLAND SCRAMBLE ON
MICK CLEARY

The face that spoke a thousand words. Andy Robinson has a fierce scowl, a narrow-eyed look of fury that has often been seen in the wake of defeat.

The former Bath and England flanker has worn that mask of anger and frustration at various times down the years. But this was different. There was something far deeper going on here, far more touching and revealing. This was the look of desolation writ large. And you couldn't help but be moved by it.

We'd seen shades of it six days earlier in Wellington when Scotland had been beaten at the death by Argentina, that fired-up, never-say-die, blue-and-white-hooped lot who have enriched successive World Cups with their passionate performances. They did so again in this pool, backed by an army of fans who sang and jumped and danced their way round the South Island in the early stages before heading to the capital city at the tip of the North Island for the Pumas' clash with Scotland.

The trip was well worth it, as was clear from the scenes of ecstasy in the rain after the final whistle had sounded on a rousing game. Argentina had somehow snatched victory – Lucas Amorosino scoring one of the tries of the tournament as he weaved his way past a clutch of forlorn Scotland defenders just seven minutes from time, Felipe Contepomi, the magnificent rallying point for a team under duress, nailing the conversion from about midway between touch and the posts. Argentina had lost two key players during the game, their incomparable No. 8, Juan Martín Fernández Lobbe, his World Cup over with a cruciate knee problem, and prop Rodrigo Roncero, yet they hung on in there and got their reward. No wonder, then, that team and fans joined in unison

▬▬ **Scrum half Ben Youngs scampers under the posts as England come from behind to beat Argentina.**

to sing for fully half an hour after the match had ended, oblivious to the sluicing Wellington rains. It was a memorable scene, although perhaps not if tartan was your fancy.

Scotland had chances, notably a duffed dropped-goal attempt from Dan Parks, a scrambled effort off the left foot with what seemed like half of Buenos Aires tearing towards him to block the shot, Contepomi typically leading the charge. The scoreline was 13-12, an unlikely-looking outcome given the way the match had unfolded. But there it was, and Robinson had to take that one on the chin.

And he did so, even though his instincts told him that Contepomi had looked offside as he rushed at Parks. In fact, later television replays suggested that the Argentina playmaker had just been supremely alert. Whatever the truth

LEFT Lucas Amorosino of the Pumas breaks Scottish hearts with his late try in Wellington. BELOW Scotland coach Andy Robinson walks by the celebrating Argentinians after the final whistle. PAGES 38-39 'What seemed like half of Buenos Aires' descends on Dan Parks as he desperately tries to get a last-gasp dropped-goal attempt away off his left boot.

clever and committed, working the field, targeting areas of frailty in the opposition and kicking the points when on offer. It had all been going to plan. Scotland hit the magical mark of 12-3 in the 56th minute, dead-eyed Paterson slotting his second penalty of the evening. They held that lead, one that would have consigned England to the unimaginable state of

of it, Scotland's defeat meant that they had to beat England, and by a margin of eight points as it turned out, or they would be out of the World Cup before the quarter-final stage for the first time in the competition's history.

Hence Robinson's face. Hence that feeling of abject misery and wretchedness writ large. Once again Scotland had made much of the running. Once again they had been

elimination, for precisely 60 seconds. That was how long it took England to restart, to claim the ball through Manu Tuilagi against a dozy Scotland line-up, to clatter forward, to recycle, and for Jonny Wilkinson, off his weaker right foot (just as he'd done in 2003 in Sydney), to pop over a dropped goal to close the gap to an all-important six points. It was a swift riposte; telling too. Scotland had let their guard drop momentarily and it was enough.

England were back in contention, and although there was over a quarter of the match to run, there was something in the Auckland air. England threw on their subs, notably No. 8 Nick Easter and, later, Toby Flood, who had the bit between his teeth as he set out to press his claim to be the starting fly half. Slowly, inexorably, the momentum of the match began to shift, not by much, but enough.

LEFT England back-rower Tom Croft rises to claim line-out ball against Scotland. **ABOVE** John Barclay (No. 7) and Alasdair Strokosch bring James Haskell to a standstill. **FACING PAGE** Delight for Chris Ashton (left) and England as the wing scores in the corner. England were through, while Scotland's hopes were shattered again.

England did leave it late before making the killer play, but make it they did. Flood surprised many in the crowd, a packed house at Eden Park revelling in the action despite the rain that was teeming down throughout, when he opted to kick for touch rather than having a pot at the posts. The score stood at 12-9, with only two minutes remaining. Flood was about 40 metres out and would have fancied his chances with a kick that was well within his range. But, no, he grabbed the ball and knocked it into the Scotland 22 for a line out. Tom Croft, the dexterous England flanker and the best back-row line-out operator in the game, rose to take the throw, England wrapped themselves round and – for one of the few occasions in the tournament, never mind the game – drove a maul with mean intent. England got position, Tuilagi banged it forward some more when the ball came back, Flood received it, spotted his man on the wide outside and didn't hesitate to throw a long, high, looped pass in the direction of Chris Ashton. The Northampton wing needed no second bidding. He scooted forward from a standing start – his speed off the mark enough to do for Chris Paterson – and his dive into the corner was a classic bit of finishing. Flood's conversion from the touch line only rubbed salt into the wound. The scoreboard read 16-12 and Scotland were out. There were still a few seconds to run down on the clock, but the die was cast: England were through and Scotland were not. It was dramatic, it was compelling and, if you were a member of the Scotland set-up, it was devastating. And that was why Robinson looked as he did.

'Thirty seconds of madness' had been his take on the previous week's loss, an apt summary of the lapse in concentration that had allowed Argentina to claim a restart and then make the play that led to Amorosino's score. And here it was again, a momentary lack of attention allowing that mid-second-half drop kick.

Robinson knew, though, that this was what England did – they found a way to win. That's not luck, that's character, savvy, self-belief and shrewdness. They may not have had many opportunities, but they made them count. They were clinical, as well as audacious, when it mattered most.

England went through to the quarter-finals unbeaten, no mean achievement. We may carp about the aesthetic quality of their play, which could be grim and fractured, but they had got to where wanted to be. They had got the job done, seen off the fiery, spirited and not inconsiderable challenges of Argentina and Scotland. They had also rattled in the tries when they had the chance, not wholly convincingly against Georgia, although a final scoreline of 41-10 is not to be sniffed at. Romania were not as stiff a task for the simple reason that they fielded an understrength side – take a bow RWC schedulers for the daft impositions placed on the Tier Two countries – and England took full advantage in scoring ten tries in a 67-3 romp. Mark Cueto, playing his first game of the tournament after recovering from a bad back, made an instant impression in bagging a hat-trick within the opening 27 minutes. Not to be upstaged, Chris Ashton then went about getting his hat-trick with his usual predatory efficiency

ABOVE Georgia giant Mamuka Gorgodze is too much to hold as he crashes over to help his country to a 25-9 win over Romania. RIGHT Mark Cueto opens England's try account against Romania. The wing would finish the match with a hat-trick. FACING PAGE Joe Ansbro has defenders falling like ninepins as he jinks to the line in Scotland's 34-24 victory over Romania. PAGES 44-45 Ionel Cazan goes in at the corner for Romania in Invercargill. The Pumas, though, were simply too strong, running out 43-8 winners.

to continue his quest to be top try scorer in the World Cup. By the end of the pool stage, Ashton was leading the way with six tries.

Even though England's outing had been relatively straightforward, they actually managed the situation with impressive aplomb. These kinds of games, when the outcome is predictable but the route towards it less obvious, can easily degenerate. Players can get lulled into glory-hunting expeditions or it can become a bit of a mess, with the opposition infringing as they fight a desperate rearguard action. So England did well to hold their shape and execute with precision.

Why then was there such begrudging praise for what they had done? They were unbeaten, had won ten of their 12 Tests in the calendar year and had scored 18 tries in four pool matches. Yet there was a perceived lack of grace about England's progress, a sense that they were unloved and unattractive. The criticism only had minor merit. True, England had been ill-disciplined, on their own admission prone to giving away too many penalties. They averaged well

into double figures on the penalty count, had had two men sent to the sin-bin – Dan Cole against Argentina and Dylan Hartley the following week against Georgia. Lock Courtney Lawes had also been cited and suspended for kneeing Pumas hooker Mario Ledesma.

But there was more, much more, to tarnish England's image. Following the opening weekend 13-9 victory over Argentina, England headed to the resort town of Queenstown for a pre-arranged five-day break from their base in Dunedin. The idea was to get some down time initially and to mix things up. They couldn't have realised just how mixed up things would become.

The scandal of a night out was to follow England right through the pool stages. Martin Johnson fended off a gentle bit of criticism for allowing his players to go bungee-jumping on the Monday following the Pumas match. That was as nothing to the opprobrium that was to come his way after pictures of Mike Tindall were splashed across the front pages of tabloid newspapers with the staple ingredient of red-top stories, a 'mystery blonde'. There were also other pictures of England players enjoying a night out in questionable surroundings. And then, just when they might have thought that they had ridden the worst of it, a Sunday newspaper splashed on a tale of a Dunedin chambermaid having lewd comments made to her by three England players – James Haskell, Dylan Hartley and Chris Ashton. The matter had been dealt with long ago, but Johnson decided to front a press conference the day after the Scotland match. Unbeknown to him at that time, another paper was running a story that Tindall had lied about where he had been that notorious night on the town.

Johnson did nothing to back away from his responsibilities that day. Several times he expressed his 'anger' regarding what had gone on. England truly were caught in the eye of a storm that they themselves had whipped up. England had also been shamed into admitting that they had changed balls during the match against Romania, allowing Jonny Wilkinson to kick with his preferred choice of ball rather than using the ball, as the laws dictate, with which the try had been scored. After a drawn-out process, two back-up coaches, Paul Stridgeon and Dave Alred, were banned from Eden Park for the Scotland match.

Wilkinson had been suffering throughout the tournament. He ended the pool stage in the incredible position of having the worst return of any kicker, with 11 misses from 20 place-kick attempts at goal.

It had been a bumpy ride for England on several fronts (Manu Tuilagi was also fined for contravening commercial regulations on mouthguards), but they were through. For all their difficulties, they were feeling a hell of a lot better than Andy Robinson.

▬▬ **Left wing Juan Imhoff dots down as the Pumas beat Georgia 25-7 in the final match of Pool B and extinguish any last lingering Scottish hopes of making the quarter-finals.**

■ Ionel Cazan of Romania puts in a big hit on Argentina's Horacio Agulla.

POOL B
ENGLAND SCRAMBLE ON
What they said...

England: Martin Johnson (coach)

■ *We made qualification hard. We got in two tough holes against Argentina and Scotland, but kept our nerve. Against Scotland we were 12-3 down, but won the rest of the game 13-0. In a gritty group we put pressure on ourselves by giving away penalties and our set-piece creaked. The game's not always beautiful. It can be chaotic and we need to handle that.*

England: Lewis Moody (captain)

■ *We didn't make it easy on ourselves with the penalty counts. We were aware of the minimum we needed in the final match, but nobody wants to go through on a losing bonus point.*

on Jonny Wilkinson's kicking form

■ *Jonny's a phenomenal player and I just love being on the field with him. He can't get all his kicks, even though you might think he can.*

Argentina: Felipe Contepomi (captain) confesses to going offside for Dan Parks's late dropped-goal attempt

■ *It was a very tough decision for referee Wayne Barnes to make, but fortunately he had his back to me and maybe he couldn't really tell if I was offside or not. Perhaps I had the benefit of being the captain and not being penalised.*

on the coming knockout stages

■ *Now we need to look deep inside us at our weaknesses and strengths to set up a game plan that suits us.*

Scotland: Andy Robinson (coach) on elimination

■ *It's gut-wrenching, but the guys gave it everything. You've got to win restarts and in the future we've got to look at that aspect. Our team tested very good opposition, but again we slipped at crucial times.*

Scotland: Alastair Kellock (captain)

■ *In the decider against England to a man we left ourselves on the park. We gave it everything we had.*

Romania: Romeo Gontineac (coach)

■ *We had a three-day recovery period before the fixture with Georgia – they had eight days. We were more tired than Georgia and it had a big effect. We got less impressive as the tournament went on.*

Georgia: Richie Dixon (coach)

■ *Other teams are more used to playing 80 minutes at this highest level of rugby. I have learned to love these boys and respect the way they want to play. I don't envisage giving up on them lightly. At the moment I have no desire to stop this.*

■ Georgia's Dimitri Basilaia in the wars against Scotland.

Putting our weight behind clients' best interests.

At Royal London Asset Management we exist for one reason - to deliver long-term investment success for our clients. This demands consistent good thinking that's well applied across all our areas of investment expertise. Equities, fixed income, property and cash.

By using our scale and reach wisely, we ensure we're always in the best place to add value for our clients.

For further information about our investment capabilities please contact:
020 7506 6500 or visit www.rlam.co.uk

royal london asset management

POOL C
IRISH STUN THE WORLD
ALASTAIR EYKYN

Ireland arrived in New Zealand recognising that they could throw the World Cup draw wide open with a single victory.

Australia were the target, but the Irish had no form to speak of. They had lost four consecutive games before flying Down Under. Their critics had been queuing up to slap them down. This was a side on the turn, they said, a tired collection of once-great players trying to squeeze one pip too many from the orange. So in classic Irish fashion, Declan Kidney's side set about proving everyone wrong.

There was little indication of the sensation to come. Ireland were unconvincing in their opening fixture against an emotionally charged USA on the tenth anniversary of 9/11. Many of the American players had been to a powerful memorial service in the morning, where several of them were reduced to tears. Both teams observed a minute's silence, and wore black armbands in remembrance of those who had lost their lives in the terrorist attacks. Inspired by the former Ireland coach Eddie O'Sullivan, the USA rattled the men in green with an obvious hunger and a ferocious defence. The Irish lacked fluidity, Jonny Sexton's kicking was off-key and their error count was high. Rory Best's burrowing try and Tommy Bowe's brace eventually saw them through 22-10.

The Wallabies had made a rather different start to their campaign in Auckland's North Harbour Stadium. Subduing a frenzied Italian pack in an opening half of two penalties each, they stretched their legs after the interval to secure a bonus point victory with a four-try blitz. Ben Alexander, Adam Ashley-Cooper, Digby Ioane and James O'Connor all scored as the Australians gave a glimpse of the slick precision and devilish adventure which had brought them the Tri-Nations crown just a couple of weeks previously. Ioane's broken thumb was the sole disappointment of an impressive first outing.

When the shock came, it fell like a thunderclap upon the tournament. It had been brewing. The USA had shaken Ireland. Romania had pushed Scotland close. Namibia had given Fiji the runaround. Wales had nearly accounted for defending champions South Africa. Still, very few thought it conceivable that Ireland could stun Australia.

More than 80 minutes are on the clock in Auckland and it's a penalty against the Wallabies. The Irish are home and hosed at 15-6.

In Auckland, hordes of green-shirted supporters thronged the streets for days before the match, intent on creating their very own southern hemisphere Dublin. There was plenty of rain in the air. The Wallabies lost their key open-side flanker David Pocock to a back injury on the morning of the game. By kick-off, they had lost their hooker Stephen Moore to sickness. The stars seemed to be aligning in a serendipitous Irish constellation.

From the outset there was a fever about the Irishmen, a confidence born of a carefully planned ambush. They launched into their vaunted opponents like men possessed. They shut down the space Will Genia and Quade Cooper so love to exploit. The front row got to work on the one area the Australians still had not fixed. Paul O'Connell remembered he was the British & Irish Lions captain. Sean O'Brien buzzed everywhere. Stephen Ferris was mountainous, at one point picking up Genia and manhandling him ten metres backwards. As a statement of Irish intent, it told you everything you needed to know.

The only jitters surrounded Jonny Sexton's boot. Despite his first-half dropped goal, his return of two successful penalties from five attempts made the Irish fans edgy. When he hit the left-hand upright in the 50th minute with the last of his efforts, they wondered if that was to be his 'James Hook moment'. Would it end up defining the night? It nearly resulted in a try for skipper Brian O'Driscoll, but the ball bounced too high from the rebound, and the Wallabies averted the danger.

Tactically, Ireland were spot on. Their defence coach Les Kiss had successfully derailed England's Grand Slam aspirations in March, pioneering the 'choke tackle'. This involved tacklers working in tandem to halt the ball carrier but simultaneously prevent him going to ground, thereby stopping the ball being released. Repeatedly, referee Bryce Lawrence had to award the put-in to the scrum to the Irish.

The plan worked, because Cian Healy, Rory Best and Mike Ross were having a field day in the set-piece. Australia had searched hard to find a pair of competent props, and their Tri-Nations victory suggested they had been successful. Ben Alexander had a torrid time, though, and Sekope Kepu fared little better. Declan Kidney had targeted the Australians' weakness, and it bore fruit in the shape of penalties. They came at a critical stage too – with 18 minutes and then nine minutes left to play, replacement Ronan O'Gara calmly

BELOW Ben Alexander becomes the first Wallaby to score a try at RWC 2011, against Italy at North Harbour Stadium, Auckland.
FACING PAGE Scrum half Conor Murray is held fast by USA captain Todd Clever as the Americans give Ireland something to think about.

notched up the six points that Ireland needed to ensure their opposition had to score twice to win.

As the clock ticked towards the 80-minute mark, the Irish try line was under siege. Genia burst forwards but was met by a wall of green. The ball was recycled repeatedly without result. With a last throw of the Wallaby dice, Cooper tried a trick pass behind his back to release either Kurtley Beale or Drew Mitchell into the corner for the try. Tommy Bowe read it, intercepted it and set off for the 90-metre race to the Australian line. Only the express pace and textbook cover-tackling of James O'Connor prevented a try to crown the Irish win. The damage was already done, however. Ireland had not only pulled off a spectacular victory against the odds, they had also denied the Wallabies a bonus point, and opened up a world of unexpected possibilities in the tournament draw.

So where did it come from, this explosion of Irish quality, power and control? There were a number of driving forces. The likes of Paul O'Connell, Ronan O'Gara and Brian O'Driscoll are proud men who had delivered a Grand Slam

LEFT With Australia on the Ireland line pushing for a try, Tommy Bowe intercepts and makes a dash for the other end. Only the corner-flagging James O'Connor (not in picture) saves a score. **BELOW** Stephen Ferris wraps up Will Genia and marches him towards the Wallaby line. **FACING PAGE, BELOW** Rory Best is tackled by Adam Ashley-Cooper but finds Brian O'Driscoll in support.

for their country and Heineken Cups for their provinces, but they had never enjoyed World Cup success. The embarrassment of the inept campaign in 2007 was fresh in their collective memory.

There were also some moving, and private, words spoken by Paul O'Connell on the eve of battle. Stephen Ferris explained that the big lock forward also had tears in his eyes as he exhorted his pack of forwards shortly before kick-off. On the day before the match, Jerry Flannery had handed out the team shirts in an emotional display. The crushing disappointment at the hooker's impending departure from New Zealand with a calf injury had struck a chord with his team-mates.

'There were some very poignant moments in the week,' said O'Driscoll afterwards. 'No more so than when Jerry handed out our jerseys. A lot of our guys won't forget that. The words he spoke were inspirational.'

It was the first time that Ireland had beaten a southern hemisphere nation at a World Cup. They had come close

LEFT John van der Giessen of the USA gathers as Hayden Smith (No. 5) and Russia's Denis Antonov compete at a line out during the 'Cold War' encounter in New Plymouth. **FACING PAGE, TOP** Anthony Faingaa drives Drew Mitchell over the line for a score against the USA in Wellington. Faingaa was knocked out making a tackle at the end of the match, but returned later in the tournament, while Mitchell's World Cup ended when he tore a hamstring against Russia. **ABOVE** The Russians celebrate as Denis Simplikevich registers their second try against Ireland.

RIGHT Martin Castrogiovanni in full flight for Italy against the USA. **PAGES 58-59** A delighted Keith Earls dives in for his second try in Ireland's 36-6 win over Italy.

before, losing 19-18 to Australia at Lansdowne Road in 1991, when the elation of Gordon Hamilton's try was snuffed out by Michael Lynagh's late score. It happened again in 2003, when David Humphreys' late dropped-goal attempt sailed wide, leaving Ireland one point adrift of the Wallabies once more, at 17-16. This time, the green-and-gold monkey had been removed from Irish backs. 'It's a good reason for a party,' said coach Declan Kidney with his customary understatement.

The result also set Ireland on course for a quarter-final place in which they were likely to avoid the defending champions, South Africa. It led to the Tri-Nations teams dropping into one section of the knockout draw and the Six Nations sides into the other.

Australia subsequently qualified for the quarter-finals as the pool runners-up, recovering from the Irish defeat with a bruising 67-5 win over the USA, in which they suffered a number of injuries. Rob Horne fractured his cheekbone, Pat McCabe dislocated a shoulder, Wycliff Palu pulled a hamstring and Anthony Faingaa was knocked out. The Americans' physicality took its toll, but the Eagles had earned the respect of many in New Zealand. They were well led by their powerhouse flanker Todd Clever, and their campaign had included a 13-6 victory in the so-called 'Cold War' match against the rising force of Russia, in which prop Mike MacDonald was outstanding.

Australia's lengthy injury list forced a shuffle of personnel and positions, but it failed to have an impact on their progress. The Wallabies comfortably saw off Kingsley Jones's Russians 68-22, in a match which saw No. 8 Radike Samo start on the wing as cover for the ailing back division. The Russians achieved the rare feat of scoring three tries against the Wallabies, as Vladimir Ostroushko, Denis Simplikevich and Konstantin Rachkov all touched down. The match featured one further Australian casualty amongst their strike runners – winger Drew Mitchell tore his hamstring and was forced to fly home.

Thanks to Australia's results and wins for Italy over the USA and Russia, the final pool match became a winner-takes-all collision between Ireland and the Italians under the roof in Dunedin. Rarely can an 'away' fixture have felt quite so much like 'home' to one team. 'It was exactly like Lansdowne Road or Croke Park,' commented Brian O'Driscoll. 'In fact I've played in Dublin in the past when the support hasn't been that good. It was incredible out there.'

POOL C *IRISH STUN THE WORLD*

The first half was gritty, bad-tempered and absorbing. In what was to prove to be Nick Mallett's final match in charge, the Azzurri pack punched its weight in the set-piece and used the rolling maul effectively. When Martin Castrogiovanni was withdrawn through injury after 36 minutes, though, the Italian challenge wilted. Ireland had a slender 9-6 lead at the break, but the platform had been established.

Soon after half-time, Tommy Bowe's incision allowed Brian O'Driscoll to run through on an inside line to touch down. Gordon D'Arcy then burst through the midfield, and once the Italian defence had been stretched, Keith Earls accepted the gift on his twenty-fourth birthday. The Munster winger's celebrations were complete when he scored his second try with the final play of the match. Moments earlier, referee Jonathan Kaplan had decided against awarding a try to Tommy Bowe after he had chased and controlled his own kick-ahead. Bowe felt he had been impeded by Tommaso Benvenuti as he tried to touch down.

A comprehensive 36-6 win allowed Ireland to qualify for the quarter-finals as the pool winners – something none of their predecessors had managed in six previous World Cups. The travelling supporters were delirious, bursting into song. Renditions of 'The Fields of Athenry' and 'Molly Malone' echoed around the Otago Stadium, which was swathed in green. 'It was a big day for Irish rugby, and how we want to be perceived,' said full back Rob Kearney afterwards. 'In terms of building a legacy, this was important. We want to create something very special, create our own history. There's a lot more to do.'

█████ Rob Kearney congratulates Brian O'Driscoll on scoring Ireland's first try against Italy at the Otago Stadium, Dunedin.

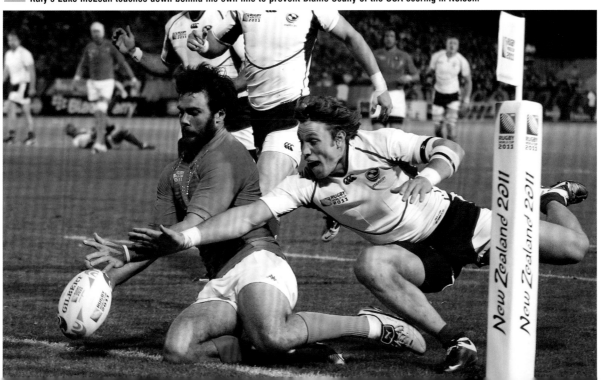

Russian wing Denis Simplikevich strides out for the line to score against Australia.

POOL C
IRISH STUN THE WORLD
What they said...

Ireland: Brian O'Driscoll (captain)

We're just very pleased we managed to get through. We didn't bring the wins in pre-tournament build-up games into the World Cup that we hoped for, but we didn't panic. I think we've managed to deliver at crucial times and we've got into a place where we're playing Wales for a semi-final spot. That's all we could have hoped for really.

Ireland: Tommy Bowe (wing)

We came out here with the ambition of winning, not to make up the numbers.

Australia: Robbie Deans (coach)

The challenge, for those who haven't been involved in a World Cup, is to learn without going through the pain. There was some pain in losing to Ireland, but we safely reached the last eight. They learned from the counsel of some of these blokes who have been here before and understand the immediacy of what they're confronted with.

Italy: Nick Mallett (coach) on his last game in charge

Obviously I am unhappy with the way we finished because I didn't think it would be so heavy a defeat in our decider against Ireland. I don't want to talk about my legacy because only history will tell if I was a good Italy coach or not. I was extremely touched by [Ireland coach] Declan Kidney, who came and said some fantastic things to me.

USA: Eddie O'Sullivan (coach)

I'm very happy with our overall performance. We set up a strategy that we'd try to get two major performances against Tier One nations and win against Russia. We certainly achieved our goal.

Russia: Nikolay Nerush (coach)

I am thankful that we managed to score three tries and a drop goal against Australia. It's been a big honour for us. Who would give up such a pleasure? Russia's first impression is that it is a great tournament. We have touched with our own hands what the Rugby World Cup is.

Italy's Luke McLean touches down behind his own line to prevent Blaine Scully of the USA scoring in Nelson.

POOL D
THE BOKS HOLD OUT
ALASTAIR EYKYN

From the moment the World Cup pools were finalised, Wales knew that they faced an almighty scrap to reach the quarter-finals.

With defending champions South Africa first up and two Pacific Island nations lurking menacingly, their campaign was fraught with danger. Samoa had recently claimed the scalp of Australia. Fiji were responsible both for Wales's ignominious exit from the pool stages of the last World Cup in France and for the humbling 16-16 draw at the Millennium Stadium in November 2010.

Coach Warren Gatland had despatched his squad to Poland during the summer. Conditions were bleak, and the fitness regime punishing. Cryogenic chambers and ice baths offered little in the way of fun, but the resilience and stamina of the players was obvious during the August warm-ups. After a patchy Six Nations campaign, these were encouraging signs of life.

Wales began the World Cup without two of their most powerful scrummagers, and their most experienced fly half.

Hooker Matthew Rees was at home, injured. Gethin Jenkins and Stephen Jones were in New Zealand, but sidelined. Gatland picked James Hook at full back for the opening game, handing the famous No. 10 shirt to 22-year-old Rhys Priestland, who had only five caps to his name, and just two starts. Seven of the Welsh match-day squad against South Africa were aged 22 or under, amongst them the captain – Cardiff's open-side flanker Sam Warburton, Wales's youngest ever World Cup skipper.

Wales's investment in youth was in stark contrast to the hard-bitten Springboks. Their coach, Peter de Villiers, was pilloried in the South African media throughout the Tri-Nations as he rested his key men. Arriving in New Zealand, he turned to his warhorses, selecting the most experienced South Africa side ever seen in an international. De Villiers assembled a record 815 caps, with 14 of the 22 players having been in the match-day squad for the World Cup final four years previously. The grizzled lock forward Bakkies Botha was the only notable absentee, through injury. The imposing figure of Danie Rossouw stepped in.

David Lemi of Samoa cannot prevent Bryan Habana from touching down for the Springboks in Auckland.

The match in Wellington began with a surge of South African power. Hook spilled the first up-and-under of the night, and after just three minutes of the game, the ball found its way to Springbok full back Frans Steyn, who crashed through the tackles of Hook and Shane Williams to score in the corner. Morné Steyn converted. The South African message was an unequivocal one.

Wales responded impressively. Warburton scavenged everywhere, and they sent their ball carriers Jamie Roberts and Jonathan Davies bursting through the midfield. Hook opened the Welsh account, and soon enough the first controversy of the World Cup was upon us.

Hook's second penalty attempt flew high into the Wellington air; so high that it cleared the right-hand upright. Neither touch judge raised his flag. The ball appeared to bend inside the post at the last moment. Or did it drift inwards after it had passed the post? Vinny Munro and George Clancy were the men underneath it. Both were satisfied the attempt had missed.

Hook asked referee Wayne Barnes to refer the decision to the television match official, but as his assistants were confident, he refused. 'I felt it went over,' Hook said sorrowfully afterwards. Gatland revealed later that Frans Steyn had told him that he agreed. 'You take the good with the bad,' said the coach. 'Good sides take disappointment on the chin and they front up next week.'

With the incident occurring so early, it is wrong to assume that the match turned on that moment. The Welsh had built up a head of steam. The Springboks lost centre Jean de Villiers to a rib injury. The half-time whistle blew. South Africa led 10-6.

After the interval, the young Welsh back row of Lydiate, Warburton and Faletau flew into the faces of their more celebrated opponents Brüssow, Burger and Spies. Faletau spilled the ball in contact just five metres out from the Bok try line but made amends after Hook's boot had put the Welsh to within a point. The No. 8's try after 53 minutes was comfortably the most important score of his fledgling career. Hook's conversion gave Gatland's charges a 16-10 lead with 27 minutes left to play.

The final quarter will take some expunging from Welsh memory banks. Reviving memories of his stunning exploits for the Lions in 2009, Jamie Roberts threw himself into the fray. Priestland looked assured. Yet there was something

■ Frans Steyn (with arm raised) is congratulated by Jaque Fourie after opening the scoring for the Springboks against Wales in the third minute of the match. By the end of the pool stage, however, Steyn was on his way home with a shoulder injury.

inevitable about a South African rally. The Boks began to swarm the Welsh, preying on their vulnerability, sensing a lack of genuine belief that they could finish the job; 815 caps said they couldn't. Francois Hougaard provided the Springbok thrust. Turning on the afterburners, the replacement winger scuttled under the posts for the decisive try. With Morné Steyn's conversion, the Springboks would squeak home 17-16.

Wales could – and should – have still won the game. Priestland's missed dropped goal from in front of the posts was the most glaring of chances. Hook drifted a late penalty well wide. No less than seven times in the match, Wales had smashed their way into the Springbok 22, only to lose possession. They had let it slip through their fingers. 'I'm proud of the effort the players put in,' said Gatland. 'We put ourselves in with a chance, but we weren't quite good enough. It's all about competing at the highest level, and that's just the little half a per cent we've got to learn.'

Rather than allowing the near miss against the defending champions to deflate them, Wales were galvanised. Knowing defeat to Samoa would send them home, they travelled to

RIGHT Three penalties from James Hook kept Wales in the hunt. He might have had more. An attempt in the first quarter was very close but was deemed to have missed and a late penalty drifted wide. BELOW Francois Hougaard, on for Bryan Habana, slices through the Wales defence to score. FACING PAGE Wales back-rower and try scorer Toby Faletau shrugs of Morné Steyn's tackle. PAGES 68-69 Namibia take line-out ball against Samoa in Rotorua.

Warren Gatland's home town of Hamilton. In a tight pool, bonus points might have proved the difference, but the destructive manner in which South Africa had put away Fiji 49-3 suggested those particular Islanders wouldn't feature in the final equation.

Wales had rested for a week. Samoa had last played just four days earlier. The playing field was far from level. Tier Two nations across the board were facing onerous schedules, thanks to tournament organisers timetabling the 'leading' countries in prime-time television slots to maximise commercial revenue.

Wales met the physical challenge of Samoa head-on. They lost Dan Lydiate to an ankle injury after only ten minutes, but two of their larger slabs of meat made their presence felt in the opening exchanges. Jamie Roberts and George North both clattered into Seilala Mapusua in the midfield, issuing a dose of his own medicine.

Wales had a clear edge in the scrum, and looked the more threatening with ball in hand, whereas surprisingly the Samoans adopted a more measured, structured approach. George Stowers was held up over the try line early on, and after half an hour the excellent Maurie Fa'asavalu burrowed over from close range. Referee Alain Rolland ruled he had crossed the line in a double movement. 'Maybe that was the turning point of the game,' muttered Samoa skipper Mahonri Schwalger later. 'I was hoping he would refer it to the TMO.'

The Welsh had been denied a try of their own. Luke Charteris butchered the chance with a forward pass to Jamie Roberts when the centre had a clear route to score. Instead, James Hook and Paul Williams traded penalties, and it was the Samoans who were pounding the Wales line with half-time approaching. Finally the tight-head prop Anthony Perenise cut inside against the defence and launched himself across the whitewash. Williams' conversion left Samoa 10-6 up at the break.

The spectre of another World Cup embarrassment at the hands of the Samoans hung heavily over the hordes of red-clad Welsh supporters. Their mood darkened when James Hook failed to appear for the second half – the victim of a shoulder injury. Leigh Halfpenny replaced him, and it was the winger's moment of magic which changed the game.

After Rhys Priestland had kicked Wales back in front 12-10, Halfpenny fielded a high ball near the left-hand touch line, just outside his 22. Somehow he ducked under the first tackle, shrugged off two more and set off on a lightning dash.

RIGHT Shane Williams calms Welsh nerves with a 67th-minute try against Samoa after front-rower Anthony Perenise had scored one for the Samoans on the stroke of half-time (FACING PAGE). BELOW Right wing Vereniki Goneva crosses for one of his four tries in Fiji's 49-25 win over Namibia.

When he found Jonathan Davies, a score looked certain, but the centre's final pass fell to earth. Fortunately Shane Williams scooped it up on the bounce for his fifty-fifth international try. 'It was one of the most important tries I've ever scored,' said the winger.

Down 17-10, Samoa made a significant final push. With two kickable penalties in the last five minutes, they hammered at the line, trying to puncture the Welsh defence, but Toby Faletau made the all-important turnover to secure the win.

The Welsh relief was palpable, and the clouds of doubt began to clear, revealing a path to the quarter-finals. 'I'm pleased with the result,' said Warren Gatland. 'I don't care about the performance. In this tournament you need luck, and you need to show character. Perhaps 12 months ago we wouldn't have won that game. It's now in our hands. We knew today it was a must-win game. Our boys dug deep. You would fancy where we are now. Possibly Ireland in the quarter-finals, then England or France in the semis. Although we might finish second, ironically it potentially favours us.'

Wales finished with a flourish, first despatching an exhausted Namibia 81-7 in New Plymouth. The Africans had been asked to perform four times inside 17 days. There was only so far their immense bravery could take them, only so many tackles Jacques Burger and his friends could make.

Fiji were next on the chopping block, and in wet conditions the precision and accuracy of the Welsh was striking as they ran out 66-0 winners. The Fijians had a forgettable campaign, the only highlight being Vereniki Goneva's historic four tries against Namibia. He became the first Fijian to score a World Cup hat-trick.

Meanwhile, the South Africans gathered a momentum of their own. After their heavy defeat of Fiji, they too dished out a thrashing to Namibia (87-0) but were given a real fright by Samoa in their final pool match. Bound tight by the desperation of potential elimination, the Islanders threw

▬▬ FACING PAGE George North on the charge as Wales overcome their Fiji frailties with a 66-0 win. ABOVE The Samoans celebrate George Stowers' try against South Africa. RIGHT Samoa's Paul Williams is given his marching orders by Nigel Owens. 'Mitigating features' contributed to the player's later being let off without a ban.

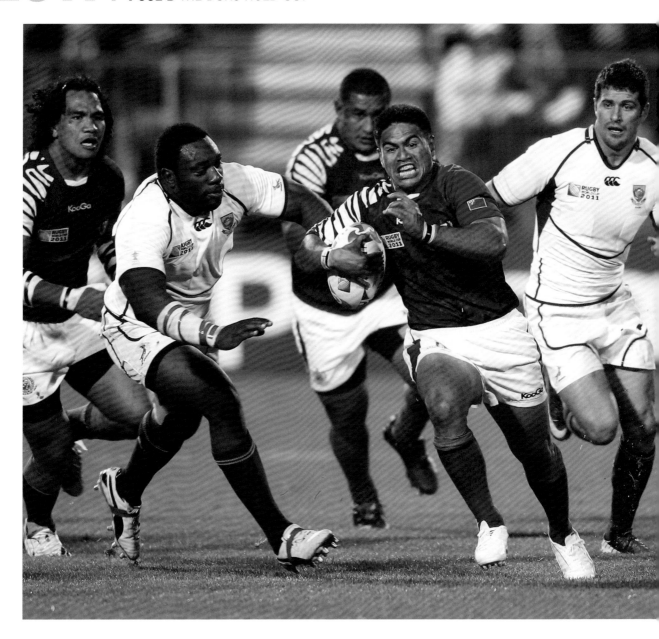

Samoa's David Lemi gives Tendai Mtawarira the slip and sets off on a searing run from his own half deep into Springbok territory.

everything at the Boks. Bryan Habana had given the defending champions an early cushion, but George Stowers' try threw the game wide open again after the interval. It triggered an all-out assault from Samoa, who caused havoc with their clever midfield wrap-arounds. Tusi Pisi and Eliota Fuimaono-Sapolu cut swathes through the green shirts.

The final half-hour was gripping as Samoa searched for a way through and both sides were reduced to 14 men. Referee

Nigel Owens turned pantomime villain as he sent off Samoa full back Paul Williams for an open-handed shove on Heinrich Brüssow. He then showed Springbok substitute John Smit a yellow card for a deliberate knock-on.

Ultimately the Samoans had left it too late to loosen the shackles that had restricted their earlier performances. The Springboks duly qualified top of the pool with a 13-5 victory, but the influential Frans Steyn was forced to fly home with an injured shoulder. The Wallabies would lie in wait for the South Africans, whilst the Welsh looked forward to a mouth-watering quarter-final meeting with a resurgent Ireland.

Jaque Fourie of South Africa is wrapped up by Samoa's Kane Thompson and colleague.

2011

POOL D
THE BOKS HOLD OUT
What they said...

South Africa: Peter de Villiers (coach)
We are labelled as a team who can't score tries. But this is how we play – we play to the situation.

South Africa: Victor Matfield (lock)
Our defence is our strong point at the moment and that's how you win tournaments.

South Africa: Bismarck du Plessis (hooker)
Defence is something we really pride ourselves on, but we still have to score tries so we can't just rely on our defence.

Wales: Shaun Edwards (defence coach)
Somebody who doesn't know the first thing about rugby would understand that our captain, Sam Warburton, is doing exceptionally well. He's very mature for his age. He's everything you want in a modern-day professional athlete: he's teetotal, he looks after his body and he's had a really strong injury-free run, which in the past he hasn't really had.

on keeping Fiji scoreless
It's rare in rugby. To get a zero you have to shoot out to a quite convincing first-half lead otherwise opponents will pick off their penalties.

Wales: Rob Howley (assistant coach)
Our wing George North is a young talent. But we look at our wings' work rate off the ball. It's not the work you do with the ball, it's the work you do without, and for him and Leigh Halfpenny, it's lines, it's physicality, it's step.

Namibia: Jacques Burger (captain) after his country's fourteenth consecutive World Cup defeat
The potential is there. Financially we are not strong enough. We play a couple of Tests throughout the year against countries – no disrespect – like Georgia and Romania. If some of our talented guys were in a professional set-up they would really wow someone.

Returning home from my club, Saracens, the England champions, it's two different worlds.

Samoa: David Lemi (wing)
I am confident that Samoa will be in top-tier rugby fighting the major nations soon.

Samoa: Census Johnston (prop)
Beating Australia earlier in the year, coming close to defeating Wales here means that we are getting better.

Fiji: Samu Domoni (coach)
To have an error rate of more than 30 in a match at this level is disappointing. We take responsibility for that. The score against Wales reflects our disappointment. It's a very young side, so it's an investment for us for the next World Cup.

Fiji: Nicky Little (fly half)
I think rugby moved on, and we did not move with it.

Namibia's Heinz Koll (centre) celebrates with Jacques Burger (right) after scoring a try against Fiji.

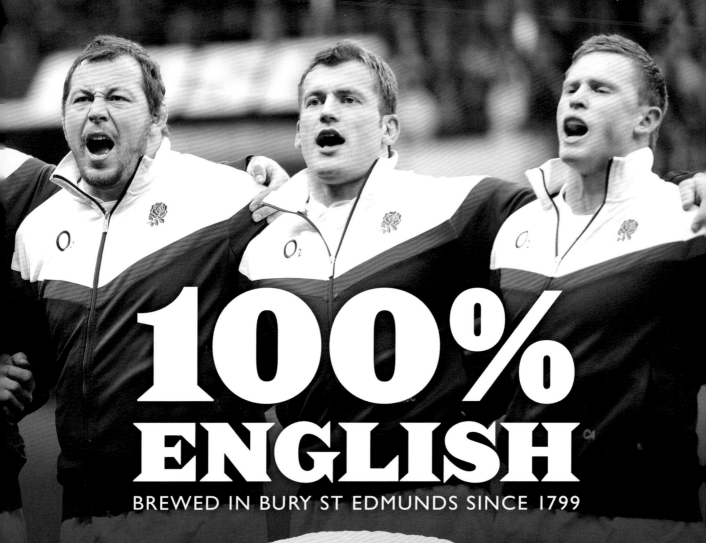

100%
ENGLISH

BREWED IN BURY ST EDMUNDS SINCE 1799

GREENE
KING
IPA

OFFICIAL BEER
OF
ENGLAND
RUGBY

ENGLAND
RUGBY

A PROPER PINT

properpint.co.uk Enjoy responsibly

QUARTER-FINAL
WALES POWER ON
ALASTAIR EYKYN

Ireland **10** | **22** Wales

The regularity of competition between Ireland and Wales has bred a familiarity amongst the players and indeed the fans, but a match of this magnitude provided a thrill on an altogether different plane.

Rarely can a rugby match have generated quite so much excitement. Celtic League meetings, Heineken Cup showdowns and even Six Nations contests all paled into insignificance when compared with a mouth-watering tie in which the prize was a place in a World Cup semi-final. In Wellington, and across the world, those of a Celtic persuasion gathered in hope, many in prayer and all in feverish anticipation of one of the great World Cup clashes.

Ireland were bidding to sail into uncharted waters. Four times they had reached the quarter-final stage of the World Cup and four times they had failed to navigate beyond. Before the match, the players spoke fondly of the accomplishments of their predecessors, whilst offering a cold-hearted reminder of their desire to carve out a legacy of their own. The colourful lock forward Donncha O'Callaghan had explained the need for this selection of European and

Grand Slam champions to 'separate themselves from other Irish teams', and leave a lasting impression on the grandest stage of all. The sensational victory over Australia, coupled with the ruthless display against Italy in the pool stage, had provided a platform for exactly that.

The Welsh ship was guided by a handful of wizened stalwarts but driven by a youthful engine of thrusting, fearless athletes. In a few short weeks in New Zealand, Warren Gatland had moulded a supremely talented collection of players into an extremely dangerous, exuberant outfit. Superbly led by Sam Warburton, they had produced some of the best rugby of the tournament. Falling in behind their leader were the young bucks like 19-year-old winger George North, centre Jonathan Davies, flanker Dan Lydiate and fly half Rhys Priestland. A new breed of dedicated professionals had emerged, and having come agonisingly close to beating the Springboks, they produced results against Samoa, Namibia and Fiji which suggested they were ready to embrace the challenge.

Wales were magnificent from start to finish. From the moment Priestland's first up-and-under landed in the grateful

Try number three coming up for Wales as Jonathan Davies powers between Cian Healy and Keith Earls and heads for the line.

arms of Jamie Roberts, there was a feeling that this was their day. In a match of breathtaking intensity, the kick led to the most spectacular of starts, with Shane Williams scooting in for a try after only three minutes. Four weeks previously, Frans Steyn had scored in precisely the same place for South Africa in their opening pool match. From that moment on, the Welsh had refused to be dictated to, and had grown in World Cup stature.

Inevitably, Wales were then forced to withstand an impassioned Irish response. Stung by the early score, Declan Kidney's troops sought the seven points which would put them on an even keel. Strong bursts from Stephen Ferris, Gordon D'Arcy, Brian O'Driscoll and Rob Kearney brought them close. Three times, Ronan O'Gara kicked penalties into touch, in search of a try from the line out, when three points were on offer from a shot at goal. The wind was swirling inside the 'Cake Tin', as Wellington Regional Stadium is popularly known. 'It's a tough one,' said captain O'Driscoll afterwards. 'The wind was a factor, and we just felt that we could keep the pressure on, and we backed ourselves to drive over the line. That cost us. We had all that time in their 22, and came away with only three points at half-time.'

The reason Ireland failed to find a way through was the cussed defence of their opposition. Tough as teak, and driven by the painful memories of two separate trips to the austere surroundings and punishing fitness regimes of Spala in Poland, the Welshmen manned the barricades. Where there was a green shirt, there always seemed to be two red ones. The back row of Lydiate, Warburton and Faletau led the way, but everyone followed. The smallest man on the pitch could be found underneath a pile of bodies to prevent Sean O'Brien scoring for Ireland after a quarter of an hour. Shane Williams had catapulted himself into harm's way, and managed to hold up the burly Irish open-side. It was a moment which epitomised the collective Welsh desire.

Wales had completed a whopping 85 tackles by half-time, compared with 46 by the Irish. Lock forward Luke Charteris had made 16 of those by himself, before injury prevented him returning for the second half. Wales defence coach Shaun Edwards had ensured that the structure was robust. He had also been working on a strategy for some weeks which involved a return to one of the fundamentals of the game – tackling the opposition low down, to prevent any momentum. 'We were trying to take the Irish feet from under

▬▬ Shane Williams is on hand to strike for Wales with the game only three minutes old. The wing touched down just where Frans Steyn had for South Africa against Wales three minutes into the Pool D match four weeks earlier.

them straightaway,' said Gatland. 'We looked at the Italian game last week, and Italy went too high against Ireland. Our focus was to go very low, and try to deny their ball carriers any go-forward. Our defence was absolutely outstanding, and it shows what good shape the guys are in. They were getting excited about defending without the ball.'

Edwards is not a man to dish out praise in a hurry, but he was purring afterwards. 'The leg-tackling was of the highest order. We've spent a lot of time in the last few months trying to reinvent the art of leg-tackling. To do that you need players with technique and courage, and we definitely had that.'

By the interval Wales had built a 10-3 lead, and Leigh Halfpenny had blasted over a 49-metre penalty. The Dragon was breathing fire, and the Irish were beginning to run out of ideas as to how to douse the flames. Ronan O'Gara twice kicked the ball beyond the in-goal area when searching for territory. It was most unlike him to be lacking in precision, but it was symptomatic of the day Ireland were having.

RIGHT It's that man Shane Williams again, this time holding up Sean O'Brien (No. 7) to prevent an Irish try on the quarter-hour. **FACING PAGE, TOP** Keith Earls squeezes in at the corner to score for Ireland five minutes after the interval. **ABOVE** Ireland full back Rob Kearney gets into his stride, only to be hunted down by Mike Phillips, Leigh Halfpenny and Toby Faletau (behind Kearney). **PAGES 82-83** Cian Healy runs into heavy traffic.

Ireland proved their resilience five minutes after the break. A poor, bouncing pass from scrum half Conor Murray inside the Welsh 22 found its way to Stephen Ferris, who popped it to Tommy Bowe. He released Keith Earls on the wing, and a textbook angled, sliding finish signalled a way back for those in green. O'Gara's touch-line conversion levelled the scores at 10-10.

A few short minutes later, though, Wales landed a killer blow through Mike Phillips. A defensive mix-up between Bowe and D'Arcy left the blind side unpatrolled, and the airborne Welsh scrum half touched down in the corner. If that try knocked the stuffing out of Ireland, the next one made absolutely sure of a historic Welsh victory. Having gently asked questions of the Irish defence, Jonathan Davies suddenly decided to have a meaningful crack at them, turned on the power and muscled his way between Cian Healy and Keith Earls to score. Priestland, who struck the post twice with penalty attempts during the evening, landed the conversion to bring the scoreline to 22-10, where it remained.

RIGHT Perilously close to the touch line, Mike Phillips dots down mid-dive for Wales's second try. **BELOW** Euphoria and despondency abound as no-side sounds.

'Those were two soft tries,' muttered O'Driscoll as he tried to explain the lapses. 'We shot ourselves in the foot.'

There was a gathering feeling of Irish desperation as the match wore on. Long-time warriors like O'Driscoll himself, O'Connell and D'Arcy recognised that their dream was unravelling, and they were powerless to stop it. For whatever reason, the fury was missing, the penetration lacking, the accuracy gone. For many of them, this would be their last taste of the World Cup. Their campaign promised so much, and finished with so little. The inspired win over Australia was magnificent in isolation, but a quarter-final exit renders it a mere footnote in the margins of history.

Declan Kidney attempted to make sense of it all, but struggled for an explanation. 'There were too many turnovers, too many concessions of penalties and two soft tries. It made life hard for us. When you give your heart and soul to something and it doesn't work out, there's just quietness. They are good men. They will bounce back.'

Warren Gatland paid a glowing tribute to the achievement of his young charges. 'Wales should be proud of these boys, of how hard they've worked. We've woken up at 5 am for training sessions, these guys went through some pain. There's no fear factor, there's a nice balance of size, of power, of loose forwards who can carry, of pace out wide. I don't want to sound arrogant, but we were confident we could win the game comfortably. They've been fantastic ambassadors off the field too, but we're not ready to go home yet.'

There was a noticeable calm about the responses to the victory from the Welsh players. They were content, satisfied with a job well done, but there was no jubilation, no over-excitement. 'We haven't won anything yet,' said their remarkably mature 23-year-old captain, Sam Warburton. He spoke the truth, of course, but Wales had secured a first World Cup semi-final place since 1987, and a fairy-tale ending was not out of the question. Grown men, tearful and clad from head to toe in red, leapt uncontrollably into each other's arms as the final whistle blew in Wellington. It was a scene replicated throughout the Principality.

■■■ A beaming Warren Gatland greets skipper Sam Warburton at the final whistle as Wales reach their first World Cup semi-final since the inaugural tournament in 1987.

■■■ Brian O'Driscoll considers what might have been, after the final whistle against Wales.

QUARTER-FINAL
WALES POWER ON
What they said...

Wales: Neil Jenkins (skills coach)

■ *Welsh rugby is proud, but for 30 years that has manifested itself in chest-puffing reminiscences. Now we face probably the greatest match in our history.*

Wales: Sam Warburton (captain)

■ *To be semi-finalists is a massive achievement on the back of an immense defensive effort from one to 15. We always say we don't start games well enough, but we began perfectly. It's a lot easier to stay ahead of the game than to chase it.*

Wales: Shane Williams (wing)

■ *When Mike went over in the corner, it gave us confidence. We're very proud of what we've done so far. Some people thought I was being funny when I said we were coming here to win it, but I wasn't. The squad contains young players, but they are experienced young players. It brings a freshness and it seems to be working.*

Ireland: Brian O'Driscoll (captain)

■ *We got outplayed in the second half, when they scored two good tries. We had a weak defence and coughed up easy scores. We needed to deliver a performance similar to those against Australia and Italy. We didn't. When you turn the ball over that many times against good opposition they make you pay. When you get to the knockout rounds of the World Cup you can't afford to play below par. We did and paid the price. We were off the pace, but you've got to suck it up when you haven't performed on the big stage. Collectively and personally I won't get this opportunity again and that really sucks.*

Ireland: Keith Earls (wing)

■ *It's heartbreaking. They were just too physical. We made some bad decisions in defence in the first few minutes and we were chasing the game.*

■■■ Donncha O'Callaghan rises above Bradley Davies to seize line-out ball for Ireland in Wellington.

Caution Caution

WOULDN'T YOU RATHER HAVE A SPECIALIST WORKING FOR YOU?

When it comes to performance and quality, you get more with a specialist. QBE is a leading business insurance specialist and proud to be the Official Insurance Partner of England Rugby and supporting The Wooden Spoon Charity. Whatever your business, we know what it takes to better manage and reduce risks. We find innovative solutions and we support you and your broker with proactive services backed by in-depth understanding. For 125 years, we've been insuring business and now we are one of the world's leading insurers and reinsurers, operating out of 49 countries with the financial strength you can rely on. For business insurance that means business, talk to your broker or visit **www.QBEeurope.com**

QBE

BUSINESS INSURANCE SPECIALIST

QUARTER-FINAL
FRANCE REGROUP
MICK CLEARY

England **12** | **19** France

One team in white, the other in black. No, not New Zealand but the colour of the cloud that hung over France as they arrived in Auckland to prepare themselves for ... what?

Well, in the eyes of many people a straightforward England victory, and into the semi-finals they go. After all, they had the hex on France in World Cups, didn't they, having beaten them at the semi-final stage in the previous two tournaments? England were unbeaten, too, even if far from imperious, on their journey through Pool B. True, they had had their off-field difficulties, ones that attracted garish headlines, but, insisted the squad, that had only served to pull them even tighter together.

And France? Well, they were a rabble, weren't they? Two defeats in the pool, the last of them to minnows Tonga in the final game, and strong rumours of divisions within the camp. Coach Marc Lièvremont had seemingly lost the support of his players after several outbursts during the pool stages. 'I don't

have a problem with what is said but with the fact that everyone knows it,' said No. 8 Imanol Harinordoquy. 'That should stay in the room and be between the coach and the player. Then he can make it public. I am not happy with this. I prefer it when the scandal stays in the room.'

The postscript to the shock loss to Tonga had been bizarre, with Lièvremont talking plaintively about how he'd gone looking for his players on Saturday night intending to share a few beers and cleanse the soul as well as the palate. Instead he found an empty room. If that gave off an image of a fractious French squad, then the reality was actually more nuanced. There had been problems, but Lièvremont actually spent the entire Sunday afternoon with his players, clearing the air over a few drinks and, if we know the French, piles of decent grub. It had been cathartic. France, far from how it looked to the outside world, arrived in decent spirits. The heart-to-heart had worked. That and the realisation that if they carried on the way they were, they would be wiped out by England.

Maxime Médard (No. 15) has just scored France's second try after half an hour of play at Eden Park.

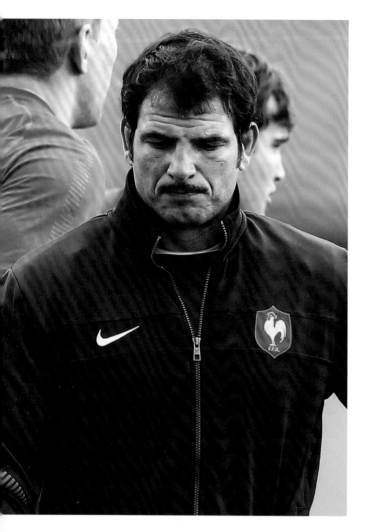

LEFT Stories had abounded of discord in the French camp and a falling-out between coach Lièvremont (pictured) and the players, but France got it together against England. **BELOW** Restored to the France starting XV for the quarter-final, Imanol Harinordoquy put in a man-of-the-match performance against *les rosbifs*. **FACING PAGE** Harinordoquy's Biarritz team-mate Dimitri Yachvili kicked two penalties to help France establish a 16-0 half-time lead.

That it was *les rosbifs* across the halfway line in opposition helped focus French minds, too. England made due claim to have taken note. But as events transpired, you wonder if they really were tuned in to what was coming their way. 'There will be a backlash,' said the France defence coach, Yorkshire-born Dave Ellis, who had been in the French camp for 12 years. 'The enemy is there right in front of you. You'll see a completely different performance on Saturday. A week is a long time in rugby, and to go from the basement to the penthouse in seven days is part of the culture of the game in France. I expect France to click.'

Ellis also stressed that Anglo-French rivalry remained as fierce as ever, born not just of those semi-final defeats but of an enmity rooted deep in the psyche of both countries. 'It's not just because this is a World Cup,' said Ellis. 'It's there because the two countries are close to each other with just the Channel between them. You see it in all sporting competitions between them. I think the rivalry is as acute as it's always been.'

One man in particular wore that enmity more obviously than any – Harinordoquy. When he was restored to the France team on the Tuesday, England ought to have been on their guard. Of course, there have been many occasions on

which the mighty Basque has not delivered for France in the same imperious manner that he so often does for Biarritz. But against England, that was something else entirely, all the more so given that his fellow *Biarrot*, Dimitri Yachvili, was there too. The scrum half with the pipe-cleaner legs may not have the look of a robust competitor, but he is certainly that, right to the core of his being. Yachvili had also done a number on England in the past, knocking over his goals with aplomb. Harinordoquy might have mellowed off the field with the passing years, but he retained the competitor's instincts on it. 'We don't have to worry about the bits of the game, we have to think only about *le combat*,' he said prior to this quarter-final.

France were certainly gathering themselves for a mighty contest. England, meanwhile, were about to embark on the biggest selection gamble of Martin Johnson's three-year tenure in charge. Having spent all season grooming Shontayne Hape as the preferred inside centre, then switching to Mike Tindall as the reliable foil to Manu Tuilagi, Johnson pulled a surprise when pairing two fly halves, Jonny Wilkinson and Toby Flood, in midfield. The sight of two playmakers alongside each other is nothing new in international rugby. It's common practice, particularly in the

BELOW Jonny Wilkinson looks to find Lewis Moody as he is hauled down by Jean-Baptiste Poux and colleagues. **RIGHT** Having spun and burst through England's attempts to tackle him, Vincent Clerc drives for the line to score France's first try. **FACING PAGE, BELOW** Manu Tuilagi, probably England's most potent weapon in the tougher matches, is brought to account by Dimitri Yachvili.

southern hemisphere. England, too, had toyed with the idea, but not for some time. They claimed that they had run the combination many times in training. That's as may be, but it was only as a stopgap.

Wilkinson and Flood had last started a Test match in that combination 18 months earlier, and then only as an emergency measure. Flood had experience there in the past but had never turned out at inside centre for Leicester.

Had Johnson arrived at this by default or design? The manager made play of the fact that Mike Tindall had been nursing a dead leg and was only just approaching full lick. Tindall, though, had been dropped – although Johnson was quick to dismiss the notion that adverse publicity about off-field shenanigans had shaped his thinking. 'If I let you guys influence what we do, then you should criticise me to the end of the earth,' said Johnson.

England were obviously looking to use the left- and right-footed kicking options to stretch France or pin them back in the corners. It was also felt that Flood's greater distribution skills might get more out of the back three of Ben Foden, Chris Ashton and Mark Cueto.

FACING PAGE, TOP Maxime Médard swivels away from the sprawling England defence before touching down to make it 16-0 to France. **ABOVE** At last something goes right for the Red Rose, as Ben Foden eludes Lionel Nallet to put England on the scoreboard. **LEFT** On for Dimitri Yachvili, François Trinh-Duc puts another nail in the England coffin with a 73rd-minute dropped goal.

As it turned out, two of that trio, Foden and Cueto, did score, but even by the time of Foden's try in the 53rd minute, the writing was writ large on the wall. England had been dreadful in the first half – truly awful, with passes scudding onto the turf rather than into the hands of the intended runner, kicks put out on the full, restarts not claimed and all manner of fretfulness in most everything that they did.

France came out as they promised, with passion coursing through their veins and steel in their defence. They were an entirely different outfit from the one that had been so bedraggled and ineffective against Tonga. They were slick, purposeful and potent within sight of the try line, as scores from Vincent Clerc and Maxime Médard within the opening half-hour showed. Yachvili had also kicked a couple of goals to make it 16-0 to France with 30 minutes gone.

England didn't really recover their composure. They did give it more of a rattle after the break, occasionally breaching the gain line, but even then the final pass was rushed and unnecessary.

Foden's try sprang from a tap penalty taken by Ben Youngs, with Simon Shaw and Courtney Lawes providing link support. It was well enough worked, but even at that stage you realised that desperation lay at the heart of England's play.

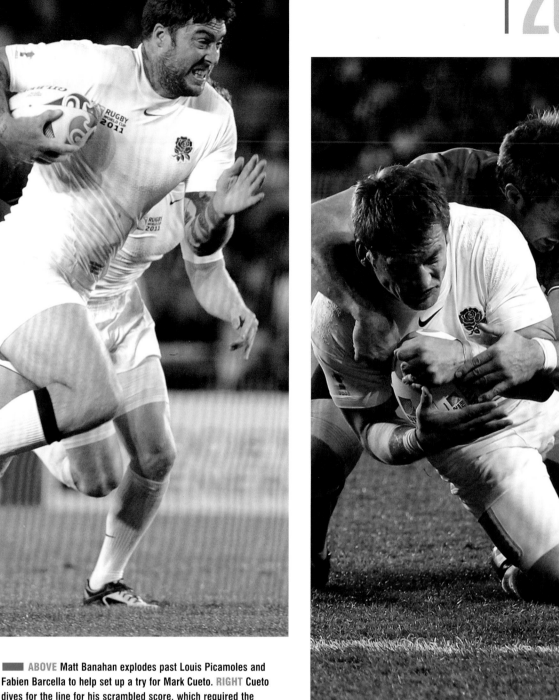

ABOVE Matt Banahan explodes past Louis Picamoles and Fabien Barcella to help set up a try for Mark Cueto. **RIGHT** Cueto dives for the line for his scrambled score, which required the involvement of the TMO.

If there was one player who summed up the malaise it was Youngs. Where was the scrum half who had looked so assured and sharp against Australia the previous year? Youngs was ragged and indecisive, clumsy round the base and self-evidently at odds with himself.

There were failings right throughout the side. The Wilkinson-Flood axis didn't really deliver great things, although there were intermittent sparks. Astonishingly they did not have one penalty kick at goal between them. There had been great mischief in the build-up, with reports suggesting that there would be some sort of shoot-out between the two to determine who would kick. That didn't materialise, nor did England on the day. Cueto's try in the 76th minute, triggered by a big bust by Matt Banahan and a slithered kick-through from Flood, did bring the difference back to seven points at 19-12, but, in truth, there was more between the teams than that.

England had barely fired a shot. This was not an irresistible France performance, summoned from the depths of their soul as it had been in Cardiff four years earlier, or sparked by their natural inclination to play with wild abandon as had happened at Twickenham, again against the All Blacks, in that 1999 World Cup semi-final. France's two tries looked slick but in reality ought to have been prevented, especially the first from Clerc, the wing managing to get past three defenders, Wilkinson, Foden and Youngs, on his way to the line. Médard's try ten minutes later saw England overcommit, three defenders targeting wing Alexis Palisson,

and the France full back taking full advantage. 'We didn't make them work hard enough for their points,' said England captain Lewis Moody. 'It would have been hard enough if France had been drop-dead brilliant.'

They weren't, but they were certainly good enough. The fallout from England's defeat, their worst performance in a World Cup since 1999, was to be long and painful. France, meanwhile, had rediscovered themselves and were into their fifth successive semi-final.

▬▬▬ **Try scorers Maxime Médard and Vincent Clerc are centre stage as France enjoy victory over England, going through to their fifth consecutive World Cup semi-final and their sixth in all. Only in 1991 did France fail to progress beyond the quarter-final stage.**

England hooker Steve Thompson rallies the troops.

QUARTER-FINAL
FRANCE REGROUP
What they said...

France: Marc Lièvremont (coach)

I feel passion, emotion. The players did what they had to do. They did something as big as other generations. One feels very much alive in such weeks, when so many things happen. I have always promised myself not to fall into bitterness. I am just enjoying simple happiness. This victory would not taste so sweet if we had played well throughout and if the English had not shown pride by fighting back … Our back row was superb. Letting Imanol Harinordoquy brood on the bench and letting him play against his favourite opponents was not a bad idea. Our first half was very accomplished. The English did not feel so good at half-time.

France: Thierry Dusautoir (captain)

We didn't want to go out in the shadow of losing to Tonga. We wanted to show how we can play rugby. I think we did. It was a great start for us. We kept the points difference comfortable during the second half. Such moments are very rare in life. We saw how much the players wanted to exist and live on.

France: Dimitri Yachvili (scrum half)

We had to cope with heavy criticism, and we showed the correct reaction. This game is about battle, about heart, and we just had those.

England: Martin Johnson (coach)

This team's best days are ahead. A lot have never been to a World Cup and this was the biggest game of their lives. So they now have that understanding and how to deal with it. Everything is amplified in World Cup knockouts and it's an eye-opener. We had poor defence. It was brutal. There were times when we could have made it easier. We didn't stop the bleeding and we were opening up the wounds. If you don't get it right at kick-off, you are in trouble.

There is nothing I would have changed in preparation. There was nothing glaring. This is not the time to discuss my future.

France's Aurélien Rougerie is halted by Manu Tuilagi.

England: Lewis Moody (captain)

A couple of lapses in defence cost us massively. France came out and performed when needed. We came off on the wrong side of that equation. It's a hard pill to swallow. We have to go away and regroup. We weren't good enough.

England: Jonny Wilkinson (fly half)

It's a painful experience. We've faced a lot of criticisms and had a lot of distractions, but it is World Cup rugby and it's hard.

England: Ben Youngs (scrum half)

Us younger players might possibly get another chance, but we feel that we have let down the older players who won't be there in 2015.

England: Toby Flood (centre)

We don't deserve to be in the semis because we didn't stand up to be accountable. I couldn't give a damn about 2015. Some won't be around next time, but those who are have to understand that you need to seize the moment.

SMALL CLUB
BIG HEART

DISSRUGBY.COM

QUARTER-FINAL
WALLABIES HALT THE BOKS
ALASTAIR EYKYN

South Africa **9** | **11** Australia

It was the perfect storm. A clash of styles, pitting muscle against movement, experience against youth, the holders against the pretenders.

There was no need for an elaborate decoding system to unearth the likely pattern of the match. South Africa would do just as every other Springbok side had done over the years and try to batter their opposition into submission. The Australians would try and absorb the rough stuff, offer greater subtlety and seek to run their ageing opposition ragged.

Both sides had endured setbacks on their path to the last eight. Australia had fallen victim to Ireland in the upset of the tournament, and their match against the USA in particular had left them with a debilitating injury count amongst their strike runners. Happily the majority of the wounded had recovered sufficiently to be available for the quarter-finals. Most significantly, the dangerous Digby Ioane was restored after hasty surgery to a broken thumb. Fellow

winger Drew Mitchell was less fortunate, hamstrung and on the plane home.

South Africa were forced to cope without two of their more potent weapons. Centre/full back Frans Steyn had seen his World Cup ended by a shoulder injury sustained during the win over Samoa. Long-standing enforcer Bakkies Botha had also packed his bags, when his Achilles tendon failed him days before the match. The notorious hard man had left many of his team-mates in tears as he spoke to them before leaving, stressing the importance of seizing the moment. Veteran winger Bryan Habana admitted to being one of those moved. 'It was pretty emotional. That guy really gave his heart to this country for ten years, and he has become a good friend. It was a bit sombre in the team room. Hopefully his ability to lift this team up will live in our hearts for quite a while.'

The New Zealand capital sparkled on match day. After a week of rain and an all-consuming blanket of grey over the city, a shiny Wellington was revealed beneath clear skies and

Springbok back-rower Pierre Spies is hammered by James O'Connor and Rocky Elsom as Australia defend for all they are worth.

LEFT Long-serving Springbok lock Bakkies Botha talks to the press after his Achilles injury forces his withdrawal from the quarter-final against Australia. ABOVE The teams line up for the anthems at Wellington Regional Stadium. FACING PAGE Wallaby skipper James Horwill crashes over in the 11th minute to score the only try of the game after the South Africans lose possession near their own line.

sunshine. South Africa fired out of the blocks the stronger. They established the tone for the set-piece battle with a huge surge in the first scrum, and they stole Australia's line-out ball. Pat Lambie and Jean de Villiers made useful incisions. The Wallabies spent their time tackling, and then tackling some more. The open-side flanker David Pocock began his work, ruthlessly scything down anything wearing a green shirt, unexpectedly snaffling possession, and reading the game beautifully – particularly the idiosyncratic interpretations of the New Zealand referee Bryce Lawrence.

Against the run of play, the opening try resulted from a turnover. The South Africans had secured their own line out, some five metres out from their try line, but Schalk Burger decided to run out of defence, when the safety of a kick to touch would have been the more pragmatic option. Pressurised by Radike Samo, Burger lost the ball in contact, and the Wallaby captain, James Horwill, burst through the defence to score. James O'Connor missed the conversion but added a penalty shortly afterwards, and Australia led 8-0.

Given the significance of the breakdown, and Pocock's brilliance, the loss of South Africa's own 'fetcher', Heinrich Brüssow, was enormously important. Just 20 minutes into the game, he was taken off, after Dan Vickerman's knee had made contact with the flanker's head at the bottom of a ruck. Despite the arrival of Francois Louw in Brüssow's place, it left Pocock free to scavenge like a hungry jackal on the African savannah. By the time he was done, there would be little left but a Springbok carcass.

The performance of referee Bryce Lawrence came under close scrutiny after the match, with the South Africans confused and angry at his leniency over Pocock's law-stretching. The flanker – along with several of his team-mates – was allowed to profit all too often from an illegal position. The South Africans were far from blameless, but Lawrence's approach meant that the key area of the game became lawless. The outgoing Springbok captain, John Smit, remarked later: 'He wouldn't listen to me, and we weren't rewarded as the attacking team. It's disappointing when the breakdowns aren't ruled evenly. The only benefit of retiring is that I won't have to be reffed by Bryce Lawrence again.'

Regardless of Lawrence's failings, Pocock did what every good open-side should and played the game right on the edge. It was a masterclass. The Australian coach, Robbie Deans, described his powerfully set No. 7 as 'immense, incredible', adding that in his view 'That was the most dominant performance of the World Cup so far.'

Despite the scoreline, South Africa were enjoying all of the possession and most of the territory. Pierre Spies and Schalk Burger went close, Bryan Habana was hauled down metres short by the offensive tackling of Pat McCabe and

FACING PAGE Man of the match David Pocock (No. 7) closes in as South African prop Gurthrö Steenkamp is stopped in his tracks. **ABOVE** Pat Lambie dives in, only for the try to be disallowed because of a forward pass. **RIGHT** Stand-off Morné Steyn drops a goal to put the Springboks ahead for the first time in the match.

James O'Connor. Morné Steyn missed a penalty from the halfway line. Fourie du Preez broke free, only to knock the ball forward as the try line beckoned. Time after time the Springboks' handling let them down, and time after time the Wallabies pounced on the ball to save their skins. Steyn eventually gave the defending champions their first points, when he landed a penalty two minutes before the break, punishing Samo's high tackle on Habana. Australia led 8-3.

The full might of the Springbok battering ram was pressed into service after half-time. It so nearly produced the goods just six minutes into the second half. Jean de Villiers found some space with a typically robust break in midfield, Pat Lambie was outside him and had a clear run to the try line, but referee Lawrence correctly ruled that the pass had gone forward. The South African frustration was palpable.

LEFT The mercurial Quade Cooper had one of his less assured periods in Australia's No. 10 shirt during the final 20 minutes of the match. **ABOVE** Watch out, Will! JP Pietersen and Victor Matfield bear down with menace on Wallaby scrum half Will Genia. **RIGHT** Adam Ashley-Cooper hurls himself after opposing centre Jean de Villiers.

At this point Quade Cooper's game became wildly erratic. New Zealand-born but Australian-raised since his teens, the fly half had been the focus of much attention throughout the World Cup, seemingly revelling in his role as the pantomime villain. His touches of genius had enlivened several of the Wallabies' pool matches, but his fragility was exposed in the final quarter of the match in Wellington. Lacking in control throughout, he'd kicked away a huge amount of possession. He punted into touch on the full, his clearances were charged down, he missed tackles and he was robbed of the ball in attack. Somehow, Australia survived.

After 72 minutes of physical, grinding rugby more associated with the northern hemisphere than their free-

ABOVE Wing James O'Connor prepares to kick Australia into the semi-finals with a 72nd-minute penalty. **RIGHT** It's all over. The Wallabies have produced a heroic defensive display to deny South Africa, making an astonishing 147 tackles to 53.

Clinging to their status as holders of the Webb Ellis Cup, the Boks pressed on, launching waves of attacks into the green-and-gold shirts. They brought on fresh legs in the form of hooker Bismarck du Plessis and the fizzing Francois Hougaard. Many in the South African press had been calling for coach Peter de Villiers to select the pair from the start. Their impact was immediate, as du Plessis charged down Quade Cooper's attempted 22 drop-out, and Hougaard used his magic feet to advance upfield.

Australia continued to defend for their lives as they saw less and less of the ball. Morné Steyn knocked over another penalty to cut the deficit to two points, and then with 20 minutes to go, from 30 metres, the fly half calmly dropped a goal to put the Springboks 9-8 ahead. It was the first time in the match that the defending champions had led.

spirited counterparts in the south, the quarter-final was decided by an infringement at the line out. As Radike Samo leapt high to collect the ball, the South African lock Danie Rossouw needlessly swiped at his opponent's leg. On the advice of touch judge Romain Poite, referee Lawrence decided it merited a penalty for playing the man in the air. All of South Africa groaned. All eyes turned towards the Australians' 21-year-old goal-kicker, James O'Connor.

Six weeks previously, Robbie Deans had disciplined the youngster for failing to appear at the World Cup squad announcement. He had overslept, and paid the penalty by missing the Tri-Nations decider against the All Blacks. Now Deans was watching nervously as the same man stood over

the ball, preparing for a kick that would decide whether the Wallabies reached a World Cup semi-final. 'He showed a lot of courage,' said Deans. 'Much of the South African approach throughout the game had been to target him, and he stood up to it. And he had the last word. The encouraging thing is that he wanted that kick, he was looking to take it. It's a great sign.'

Ice-cool, O'Connor drilled the ball straight between the posts. Shortly afterwards, scrum half Will Genia kicked it dead after one last scrum, and Australia were into the last four with an 11-9 victory. It was the rugby equivalent of Muhammad Ali's 'rope-a-dope' tactics against George Foreman in the 'Rumble in the Jungle' in 1974. The Wallabies

Springbok skipper John Smit, on his way into retirement, congratulates David Pocock, the Wallabies' supreme ball winner, after the final whistle at Wellington Regional Stadium.

had allowed South Africa to punch themselves out. They had spent the whole match feeding off scraps but delivered the knockout blow to the defending champions. The statistics made for remarkable reading. South Africa enjoyed 76 per cent of possession, 56 per cent of territory and made just 53 tackles compared with 147 by the Wallabies.

'The mood in our dressing room is three notches lower than a funeral,' said South Africa's coach, Peter de Villiers, afterwards, during a curious press conference in which he appeared to resign his position. 'We didn't take our chances. They took theirs. It's been a brilliant journey, but the journey

for me is over.' His retiring captain, John Smit, agreed. 'We needed those special moments to go our way and they didn't. It's the first time I've lost a game on the scoreboard, and won it everywhere else. It's sad, having dreamed of the fairy tale. It's the end of a chapter, but I've been blessed to be captain of the Springboks.'

Robbie Deans was relieved his men had found some way to win. 'It takes a lot of guts to get a result in games like that. We always like to play with the ball in hand, but you have to adapt, and that's a good skill to have. It's not just about the perceived beautiful things we do with the ball. What you saw out there was the most experienced side in the world turn the screw on the youngest. The boys came of age, the way they accepted that challenge.'

Springbok coach Peter de Villiers, who stood down after the game, soaks up the atmosphere one last time.

QUARTER-FINAL
WALLABIES HALT THE BOKS
What they said...

Australia: Robbie Deans (coach)

We saw an epic World Cup encounter. Different, but that's what makes this game what it is.

on David Pocock

The world is blessed with some very good 'snafflers' and he is among the most productive.

Australia: James Horwill (captain)

Not everything went our way but one thing you can't teach or train is effort and commitment from the group.

Australia: James O'Connor (wing) on the place-kick that sealed victory

That moment has not stopped running through my head.

The Wallaby defence stands fast, driving back yet another South African charge, led this time by flanker Schalk Burger.

South Africa: John Smit (captain) who was retiring

It's not important how I want to be remembered. People always talk about a legacy, but I would be proud to know that in future those who played with me will ask what would Smitty have done, on and off the field. If that's the case I will be happy.
We have had a great four years together and that has been pioneered by our coach Peter. Not the usual mould of coach, but one that we have thoroughly enjoyed. His saying from the day he started is that even the bad days are good. He has made us enjoy every moment. He's given us leeway and space and he's tightened up when we have taken advantage. A great man.

South Africa: Jean de Villiers (centre)

We have only ourselves to blame. Sometimes you get one or two opportunities and you need to take them, and Australia did that. We didn't deserve to win.

Yet another *formidable* team.

A GROUP OF very different individuals. Each with a specialist skill. Yet all part of the same team, sharing a common goal. Sound familiar? Indeed doggedness, discipline, intense concentration and effort are all elements that are just as important on the Profit hunting grounds as they are on the rugby pitch. If you'd like to find out more about Hunting Profits why not get in touch? You'll find our contact details below. Please remember that past performance should not be seen as a guide to future performance. The value of any investment and any income from it can fall as well as rise as a result of market and currency fluctuations and you may not get back the amount originally invested.

Fig.1: A typical PROFIT

ARTEMIS
The PROFIT Hunter

QUARTER-FINAL
BLACKS PASS PUMA TEST
MICK CLEARY

New Zealand **33** | **10** Argentina

Could it possibly be? Could the greatest upset in World Cup history actually be taking place? Felipe Contepomi's conversion had just made it 7-6.

It certainly had many thousands on the edge of their seats, nervously nibbling nails when Argentina flanker Julio Farías Cabello picked and plunged over the try line on the half-hour mark, much to the joy of the delirious throng of blue-and-white-bedecked Pumas fans in the Eden Park crowd. Sure, there had been only 30 minutes played, there was a long way to run on the clock; once the boys in black got into their stride, it was going to be fine, wasn't it? Those New Zealanders of a really twitchy disposition might have had their anxiety levels pricked by a perusal of the pre-match stats, which told them that the All Blacks had scored a try in 93 Tests in succession.

So where on earth was this evening's customary score? It didn't come for a long, long time; not until Kieran Read's touchdown in the 66th minute. Instead of tries, it was the unfamiliar boot of Piri Weepu that kept the All Blacks on the move on the scoreboard. Weepu was not quite a makeshift kicker for he is a fine all-round footballer, but he'd had to step forward once Dan Carter had fallen prey to injury.

Ah, dear Dan. How New Zealand had been traumatised in the build-up to this quarter-final. The pictures of a stricken Carter had gone round the world, never mind the country. The darling of the Kiwi masses – the supreme player of his generation and nudging those in the pantheon of all-time greats for inclusion – had cut a tragic figure as he lay curled up on the turf after collapsing in pain as he took a routine kick in a training session the previous weekend.

Carter knew there and then that it was all over. The rumours spread like wildfire. The unimaginable had actually happened. Carter Was Out. The Nightmare Had Arrived. Black Day for Blacks. The World Cup Project In Tatters. You had to do a double take to remind yourself that this was just one player of many who had been injured. Just as pivotal, perhaps, was Pumas No. 8 Juan Martín Fernández Lobbe, who had been invalided out of the tournament during the Scotland game. But there were few headlines on Lobbe.

■ **Jerome Kaino runs at the Argentina defence as the All Blacks have to work hard for their win at Eden Park.**

Carter's injury brought the country to a standstill. The worst news was confirmed on Sunday, and Carter addressed the nation the following day, live on television. Yes, that's a rugby player, not the prime minister. Actually, it's not fair on Carter himself to dramatise it too much, for he himself recognised it for what it was worth – one of those things in sport. Yes, he was devastated, traumatised even, but injury was a curse lurking in the shadows, a curse of which all sportsmen were wary.

Carter put on his best face for the cameras. 'I knew it was pretty serious because of the pain,' he said. 'I was actually having a bit of a shorter session than usual. I normally kick a good 15, 20 balls at captain's run, but I was only having four this time around.

LEFT In the absence of Dan Carter, scrum half Piri Weepu had taken over the goal-kicking, biffing over seven penalties against the Pumas. **BELOW** The All Blacks lose another fly half as Colin Slade (left), in for Carter, goes off injured and is replaced by Aaron Cruden.

'It was my fourth kick and I didn't know what happened. For something like this to happen has been really tough. I can't put my finger on why. I'm constantly asking "Why did this happen?" I don't have the answer, unfortunately.'

Given the number of balls a kicker will bang between the posts during a run-of-the-mill session, there was something particularly resonant about the fact that Carter was kicking

only four balls, and it happened on the fourth pot. Fate really was out to get him.

'Lying in bed on Saturday night was pretty tough, looking back at one of the craziest days of my life. To be named All Black captain – something very special – and to have that taken away from you through an injury and then later to find out that my dream of being involved in the World Cup was now over. It's pretty gut-wrenching and disappointing what happened, but I have to get over that and continue to think positively and try to help the guys in whatever way I can.'

The All Blacks knew that they had to move on pretty damn quickly, not mope and curse. Yet there was more tricky news in store, from newspaper stories of wing Cory Jane being caught late-night drinking just three days before the match, to injuries during the game itself. Carter's back-up, Colin Slade, stepped into the starting No. 10 shirt, with Manawatu fly half Aaron Cruden drafted into the squad. It wasn't long before Cruden was in action himself, replacing Slade after 33 minutes of the quarter-final. Slade, would you believe, had also succumbed to a groin injury. Exit stage left, Carter and Slade. Enter stage right, Cruden (and, later, Bath-bound fly half Stephen Donald, summoned as cover for New Zealand's dwindling fly-half resources). Twenty-two-year-old Cruden was regarded as a fine prospect. We were about to find out if promise could turn to substance. It could.

███ **ABOVE** Veteran Pumas hooker Mario Ledesma hauls down Ma'a Nonu. **FACING PAGE, TOP** Leonardo Senatore passes Richie McCaw and roars away to create a try for Argentina. **LEFT** The move ends with Julio Farías Cabello hurling himself over the line to score.

QUARTER-FINAL *BLACKS PASS PUMA TEST*

Cruden looked the part. Slade had appeared edgy, aware of the mantle he was assuming. Cruden just got on with it. He was sharp, elusive and decisive. The King is dead! Long live the King!

It was Weepu, though, who really ran the show, from the moment he led the haka until the time he left the field in the 73rd minute, job well and truly done. He'd only missed one kick – the conversion of Read's try – in amassing 21 points from seven penalty goals. It was 26-10 when Weepu gave

BELOW Mils Muliaina (No. 15), Leonardo Senatore (right) and Gonzalo Camacho contest a high ball. **RIGHT** Having had a first-half effort disallowed for a foot in touch, Kieran Read gets over the line to score the All Blacks' first try after 66 minutes.

way to Jimmy Cowan. The Pumas had been resolute, fierce and unrelenting, but they just didn't have enough strike power to make a difference. Brad Thorn's try, and Cruden's conversion, in the 78th minute gave an unfair spin to the scoreboard. The All Blacks had been in a rare old scrap and they knew it.

The Pumas had been worthy opponents, had tested New Zealand's mettle on all fronts. Their try had been a gem. Leonardo Senatore, a part-time professional who plied his trade back home in Argentina, blasted off the back of a scrum, darting inside the supposedly accomplished back-row duo of Read and McCaw, and steamed downfield. When the 27-year-old was hauled down on the New Zealand 22, he found plenty of mates in support. A delicious flip onwards by Contepomi kept the move going. Even though the All Blacks had scrambled back in numbers and seemingly stemmed the advance, Cabello had the presence of mind to pick up and blast his way over.

Argentina suffered in the penalty count and had scrum half Nicolás Vergallo sin-binned midway through the second half. It had been a mighty effort, with outstanding contributions from lock Patricio Albacete, flankers Cabello and Juan Manuel Leguizamón, and, naturally, from Contepomi. It would probably be the last time we saw the Argentina skipper at a World Cup. It was certainly the last we would see of 38-year-old hooker Mario Ledesma. He was hugged and applauded by his team-mates on the bench as he was replaced in the 70th minute, a true warrior.

'Everything I experience from here on will be banal compared with what I have lived through these past 16 years,' said Ledesma. 'It was my dream as a kid. I wanted to enjoy every minute and I did right down to the last kick. Personally, that was my best match of the World Cup.'

It was that. But New Zealand had prevailed. Head coach Graham Henry was asked afterwards what it felt like to be in a World Cup semi-final. 'Bloody amazing, never been in one before,' he said, with an ironic quip about the anguish caused by the quarter-final exit four years earlier. Henry was

FACING PAGE Cory Jane shows great skill to keep the ball in play while under pressure from three Pumas tacklers, including Santiago Fernández (No. 10), enabling the pursuing Brad Thorn to canter in and score the second New Zealand try (**ABOVE**).

generous in praise of the opposition, noting that they would be a great addition to the Tri-Nations.

The All Blacks had not quite hit their straps but would be much the better for the testing experience. The controversy surrounding Jane's off-field indiscretions, which had only broken that morning, was swatted aside by Henry. New Zealand manager Darren Shand had stated that Jane had better play well. He did, with some forceful running along the flanks.

There was heartache as well as joy for full back Mils Muliaina on the occasion of his 100th cap. There was a very moving presentation of his commemorative cap by Jock Hobbs, Muliaina wincing as he leant towards Hobbs, knowing already that a blow sustained to his shoulder during the game was serious. It was. He was out. There was also continuing concern over the foot injury that McCaw had been carrying.

ABOVE Mils Muliaina is applauded from the field by both sides after a post-match ceremony in which he was awarded his 100th All Black cap by Jock Hobbs. Sadly it was the end of the tournament for Muliaina, who had picked up a shoulder injury during the game.
LEFT Pumas skipper Felipe Contepomi waves after the final whistle of what was possibly his last World Cup match.

The All Black captain made it through but without looking anything like being at his best.

The Pumas themselves were realistic. New Zealand's level of performance was still that notch above theirs. 'I think it was competitive for 60 minutes, then I think the All Blacks showed their magic and they won well,' said Contepomi. 'In the first hour we managed to control them but then they kept coming at us and that's where the difference is between the two teams. When you play them it's like a black wave coming over you and it's hard to stop them.'

The black wave was headed for the semi-finals; Argentina for home.

■ Pumas skipper Felipe Contepomi puts boot to ball as he is challenged by All Black centre Conrad Smith.

QUARTER-FINAL
BLACKS PASS PUMA TEST

What they said...

New Zealand: Graham Henry (coach) on being in a World Cup semi-final for the first time

■ *I'm very happy. I thought it was a good, tough old game of football. Piri was outstanding. He kicked superbly. Mils is a top man, a great guy. He deserves all the praise he gets.*

New Zealand: Richie McCaw (captain)

■ *The way it turned out was the expectation we had. We did really well at the set-piece. Even though it came close a few times, we realised we had to stick to it and take chances and that's the way it turned out.*

■ *Argentina are a team who attack the breakdown well and they slowed our ball down in the first half, so that was one of the improvements for us in the second half.*

■ *It's just great that Mils got out there for 100 caps. He's just a champion. Shame to see he got an injury, but he hit that milestone.*

New Zealand: Piri Weepu (scrum half)

■ *They managed to slow our ball down quite a bit and we knew what they were capable of. We just had to ride the storm and play the full 80. I am just grateful and humble to be here.*

New Zealand: Mils Muliaina (full back) who was winning his 100th cap

■ *Being told I would run the boys on made me pretty emotional, but All Blacks don't cry, so I did my best not to.*

Argentina: Santiago Phelan (coach)

■ *We came here to grow as a team. We had highs and lows. This team is young and has a great future. Even though we were beaten, we were proud of the players. We were playing the best in the world. For Argentine rugby, it was important to reach the quarter-finals. It will be very important for us to play teams of* this calibre every year in the Four Nations. We will grow.

Argentina: Felipe Contepomi (captain)

■ *Our strong defence is a big part of our game. We need to improve the other basic skills. When we have the ball, we have to try to keep it a bit longer because we have some players who can play dynamic rugby. But that will happen when we play each year against the best. I know I can go into the dressing room and look everyone in the eye. Obviously we are not happy to lose, but overall it was a good tournament. We all worked together.*

■ Argentina stand-off Santiago Fernández grapples with Sonny Bill Williams, who was selected on the wing for the quarter-final.

IT'S TIME TO SEE WHO IS MADE OF MORE

ESTD 1759
GUINNESS

GUINNESS

SEMI-FINAL
BRAVE WALES BOW OUT
MICK CLEARY

Wales **8** **9** France

The moment that referee Alain Rolland reached for the red card, Wales's World Cup dream was over. As Sam Warburton trudged towards the touch line, he probably knew that. Blown it. In one rash moment.

A tackle. One measly tackle. Well, it was anything but measly, but four years of work, money, sweat, toil, heartache, setbacks, recovery, problems, emotional investment, hope and expectation were all distilled into one bloomin' tackle.

Of course, Rolland has to be pilloried for such a swift, knee-jerk response to the tip tackle on France wing Vincent Clerc. He should have drawn breath. He should have consulted with his touch judges. He should have awarded yellow. Rolland should have done all of these things. But he didn't. He opted for the letter of the law. Warburton was on his way to the sidelines with only 18 minutes played of the World Cup semi-final, a game watched by millions round the world and by many thousands of Wales fans who had paid vast sums of money to be there in person. Rolland took no note of these factors. He'd seen the tackle and made his call.

It was red. That's what the law book says he should do and that's what he did.

Warburton was no innocent in all this. Much as many took issue with Rolland for being too rigorous, too pedantic, too unfeeling, ruining what was shaping up to be a great contest, fault also lay with the Wales flanker. All players know that the IRB has cracked down on such tackles. They know the risk. Of course in the split-second moment of impact, in that tiny splinter of time available to size up the opponent, how do you decide how you're going to tackle him? Well, Warburton drove hard and upwards. Clerc was off his feet in an instant and quickly on his way down, thudding into the Eden Park turf. By this time, Warburton had realised what was going on and had partly released his opponent. Too late. The damage was well and truly done.

There was a minor scuffle between players from the two teams, there was a moment of almost stillness as Rolland reached into his pocket, followed by growing shock as the implications of the entire incident began to sink in.

Clerc was back on his feet within a minute or two. The game itself never recovered. And for that, we can blame

▬▬ **France hooker William Servat makes a break and finds himself in open water at Eden Park.**

both Rolland as well as the French team. Instead of embracing the advantage with assured abandon, looking to exploit the fact of having an extra man by running Wales off their feet with a passing game, France became petrified at the prospect. They played like a bunch of scaredy-cats, cramped and fretful, kicking ball away rather than looking to work the field and tire out Wales. It was truly dispiriting stuff, an abnegation of the values of the game and a betrayal of France's glorious heritage.

Somehow Wales hung in there, stunned by losing their captain and open-side flanker. It gradually dawned on them that France had completely lost focus. They were there for the taking. If only. If only, eh? Much as Warburton's sending-off shaped the flow of the game, Wales still had chances, great chances, to pull off what would unquestionably have been the greatest victory in World Cup history.

Wales scored the only try of the match – and what an indictment of France is that statistic – through Mike Phillips in the 59th minute, the scrum half arcing past the outstretched

RIGHT Lionel Nallet soars above Luke Charteris to win the ball for France at an early line out. **BELOW** Eighteen minutes in and Sam Warburton upends France wing Vincent Clerc, who crashes to earth. **FACING PAGE, BELOW** Mr Rolland produces the red card, consigning Warburton (partially hidden by No. 8 Toby Faletau) to the sidelines and Wales to an uphill struggle.

clutches of lock Pascal Papé to touch down halfway between the posts and the touch line. Ought Phillips to have got closer to the posts? Perhaps, although France wing Alexis Palisson was covering across fast. As it was, it was still a relatively straightforward conversion for a kicker of Stephen Jones's calibre. Jones, playing in his 103rd Test, had come on for James Hook, himself a stand-in for the injured Rhys Priestland, in the 46th minute. This was his first place-kick of the match. The score was 9-8, Morgan Parra having kicked all his goals for France. Nudge the conversion over, and 14-man Wales, improbably, gloriously, would be in the lead. But Jones duffed it, the ball pulled slightly off-centre and clipped the nearside post. The conversion was not a gimme, but nor was it difficult.

▬▬▬ **LEFT** Imanol Harinordoquy tidies up for France at the base of a scrum. **FACING PAGE, TOP** Toby Faletau charges forward as Wales pound incessantly at the French door in the final quarter. **ABOVE** With Dimitri Yachvili bearing down on him, Stephen Jones tries a dropped goal off his left foot, but with no joy. **PAGES 130-131** Mike Phillips takes to the air to score for Wales as Alexis Palisson, too late to stop the try, forms a barrier between Phillips and the posts, crucially making the conversion that bit more difficult.

It seemed a bad miss at the time. And its significance grew with each passing minute. Wales became more and more prominent the longer the game went on, an extraordinary state of affairs given that their line out had crumbled and that they had lost influential tight-head Adam Jones with a torn calf only ten minutes into the match. France were dreadful, incapable of putting any phases together, without soul or ambition in their play.

But they hung on for all they were worth. As the clock ticked down, so the tension rose. Surely Wales must score something, anything. Jones appeared to fluff an opening by not dropping for goal when he should have done so and then rushing another attempt and making a hash of it.

Wales were rueing these opportunities. Hook had missed two decent penalty-goal chances in the first half before he was replaced. Then, in the 76th minute, the sight of France

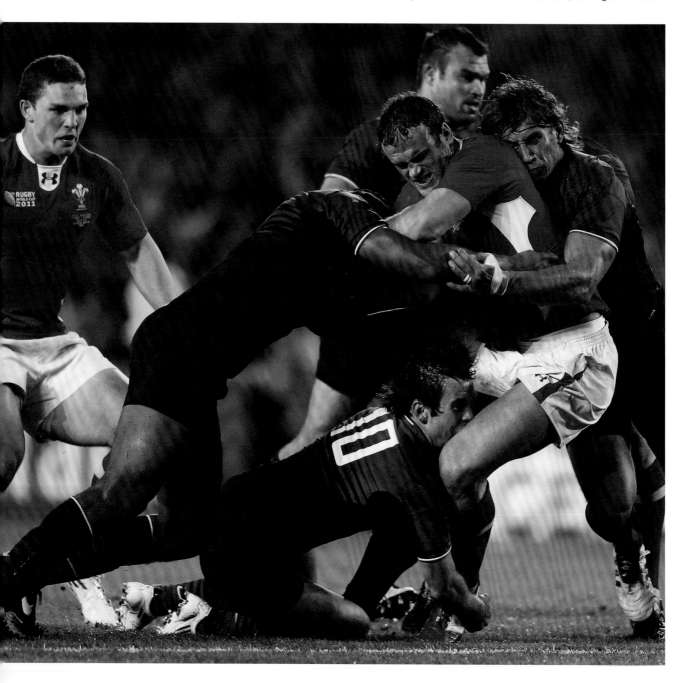

tight-head Nicolas Mas with his head in his hands was enough to tell you that he'd given away a penalty. Chance to Wales. It was long-range, pretty well on halfway. Up stepped full back Leigh Halfpenny, a small man with a mighty boot. This was the moment he'd dreamed of for years. Prior to the match, Halfpenny had spoken movingly about how his grandfather had taken him to the local playing fields and helped him practise his kicking as a small boy. Here was the moment when that devotion and dedication might pay off.

Well, Halfpenny almost made it. But close, the ball just dipping under the crossbar, is not close enough. France had escaped again. And they were to again in the very last sequence of the match, when Wales went through 27 phases but simply could not manoeuvre either of their kickers into position for a drop at goal. We all thought that Jonny Wilkinson's drop for glory in Sydney in 2003 had been a routine bit of work. Here was proof that it was anything but. Sure, Wales only had 14 men, exhausted men at that, but even so, France's discipline was impeccable as they rebuffed attack after attack. Finally, a mistake came, Jamie Roberts losing control in contact. The ball was turned over, allowing Dimitri Yachvili to belt it high into the stands.

And then the recriminations began.

To be fair to Wales, they kept a lid on their anger. Well, for the most part.

'I thought France were really poor, and I thought it was the wrong decision by the referee to send Sam off,' said Phillips. 'It was the wrong decision completely. He is a young kid, he is the captain of his country, it is the semi-final of the World Cup. He is not a dirty player. He's a big hitter and that is what happens. It was a yellow card and that's it. It was just the wrong decision. It looked much worse than what it was. It was early on in the game, it is a massive game, you are flying into each other. You put big hits in and people go up in the air – that's the way it is. France played up on it. It was showmanship, and they did their job. It is just disappointing.'

As for France, coach Marc Lièvremont made absolutely no apology for the manner in which they had played. 'I don't give a damn what people think of us,' was the coach's opening remark at the press conference. 'We have won and we are in the World Cup final.'

The ends justified the means as far as Lièvremont was concerned. Well, that was a narrow view, as well as a distorted one. Playing 10-man rugby as Argentina had done in 2007 is fine: it's a strategy based on particular strengths and still has to be well executed. In this instance, France were craven and cowardly.

Lièvremont was having none of it, and had little sympathy for Wales's plight, either. 'Our players have been amazingly brave but the French team might have a good guardian angel,' said Lièvremont. 'You have seen the tackle, it was a very dangerous tackle and it deserves the red card but it was unfortunate that the game was unbalanced in the way it was.'

There was to be no backing down from the International Rugby Board, who endorsed Rolland's decision. An IRB spokesman said: 'Regular directives to unions, match officials and judicial officers have been issued in recent years reinforcing the IRB's zero-tolerance stance regarding dangerous tackles and the promotion of player welfare.'

There were tears from several Wales players, as well there might have been.

'I thought the kick was there,' said a stricken Halfpenny. 'I did not hit it quite properly but I still thought it was going over. It was not the best strike but it was on target. I have put in a lot of work into my kicking over the years and it all came down to that moment. It kills me talking about it.'

His grief was shared by many. France had won a World Cup semi-final not through their own magnificence or grandeur but through a refereeing decision made effectively in a committee room and not on the field of play. Halfpenny was not alone in his tears. The game was weeping too.

▬▬▬ The anguish of defeat for Shane Williams and Wales, while in the background France rejoice as the no-side whistle puts them in the World Cup final.

Wales wing George North is held up by Maxime Médard and Vincent Clerc of France.

SEMI-FINAL
BRAVE WALES BOW OUT
What they said...

France: Marc Lièvremont (coach)

I think there are a lot of people annoyed that we have qualified ... In the final phases the Welsh were still 45 metres away, so I was quite serene. When they went down to 14 we were inhibited. We were not daring. Their loss made us nervous and that was the paradox. We had a narrow escape and we are privileged.

on the France squad

I asked them not to go out after the match and some of them did. I told them that they were selfish, undisciplined, disobedient spoilt brats, always complaining, always whining and that for four years they have been on my case.

But it is really not that important. In the end a cigarette, a dessert after dinner or a couple of drinks will not affect how you play in the final. I also told them that I have a lot of affection for them, but it is a shame that they don't look after themselves.

France: Dave Ellis (defence coach)

Morgan Parra made 14 tackles. He is a great No. 10. Towards the end we were very disciplined. The last sequence had more than 20 phases and we prevented them making any progress.

France: Thierry Dusautoir (captain)

We won thanks to our defence. We didn't play rugby, but we played with our heart. When they scored the try and when the conversion was being prepared we were scared.

Wales: Warren Gatland (coach)

Sam is not a dirty or malicious player. So what's the point of an experienced referee spoiling a semi-final by giving red with such a quick decision? We were one down against world-class opposition and the fact we had a chance to win shows the character of our players.

We accept that Sam lifted him and it probably warrants a yellow under the referees' instructions. But he let him go; he didn't drive his head into the ground. The wing was fine to carry on.

Wales: Shaun Edwards (defence coach)

I think it's a travesty for the competition because clearly the team who should be playing in the final aren't going to be. I am empty. In the opinion of the rugby world we should be there. It was not deliberate. It deserved a penalty and potentially a yellow. But Sam is world-class and should be in the World Cup final ... I have seen and received deliberate spear tackles. It is horrible. With Sam, it was a dominant hit. He was much more powerful than the guy he tackled.

Wales: Sam Warburton (captain)

There was nothing malicious. It felt that as soon as I hit him his body weight took control. I went to compete for the ball, thinking it was a normal tackle. The next thing I'm walking off. The boys are gutted, but I thought the courage and bravery they showed was second to none.

Wales: Shane Williams (wing)

There's no use blaming Sam. It knocked us for six. We were knackered by half-time. Not conceding a try with only 14 men was a tremendous effort. There was a lot going against us, with Adam Jones going off as well, it wasn't our day.

I told Sam that he's a great player and if it weren't for him we wouldn't have come this far.

Dismissed Wales skipper Warburton can only watch and hope.

100% ENGLISH

BREWED IN BURY ST EDMUNDS SINCE 1799

GREENE KING IPA

OFFICIAL BEER OF ENGLAND RUGBY

A PROPER PINT

properpint.co.uk Enjoy responsibly

SEMI-FINAL
BLACK BLITZ
MICK CLEARY

Australia **6** | **20** New Zealand

How could we have doubted them? How could we have thought that Australia, the Tri-Nations champions, might send a nation heading towards the cliff edge by denying the All Blacks their rightful place in a World Cup final?

Of course, the very fact that the Wallabies had won the annual battle of the southern hemisphere, or that they would not be fazed by a black shirt across the halfway line, or that New Zealand had been less than overwhelming in their quarter-final win over Argentina, might have led you to that conclusion. Factor in too that the All Blacks were down to their third-choice fly half in 22-year-old Aaron Cruden, the skateboarding kid from Palmerston North, who was surely liable to freeze on the big stage. You could scratch around for other reasons as to why the All Blacks might have been on shaky ground. Might this not be the night that New Zealand-born Wallaby fly half Quade Cooper, Public Enemy No. 1 for his heinous crime of giving Richie McCaw a few verbals and

a bit of a nudge in previous encounters, might actually come good and torment the opposition?

Dream on. From the moment that the aforementioned Cooper, more liability than magician, booted the ball out on the full from the kick-off, there was only going to be one winner. The All Blacks were irresistible, giving their most complete performance of the tournament by some considerable distance. From that first restart scrummage on, they delivered on all fronts: resolute and productive in the forwards, innovative and potent across the back line. It was as if someone had flicked a switch to set the backs in motion, with the dial flicked to superfast every time a bloke in black got the ball. The Wallabies are no slouches when it comes to slick-heeled back play, but across those opening exchanges they could barely lay a finger on their opposite numbers. True, they themselves were missing their own primed missile, full back Kurtley Beale, whose injured hamstring hadn't quite healed, but even so they would have struggled to match the All Blacks even with a full complement.

All Black wing Cory Jane makes one of many magnificent aerial takes, this time under pressure from Digby Ioane.

ABOVE David Pocock takes the ball into contact. The flanker was prominent as the Wallabies manned the barricades against the marauding All Blacks. FACING PAGE, TOP Stephen Moore (No. 2) and Sekope Kepu bring down Richard Kahui. RIGHT Ma'a Nonu latches on to Israel Dagg's pass and crosses for New Zealand with six minutes on the clock.

No matter who had the ball, there was immediately an edge to New Zealand's play, from the strong-arm scrummaging of the likes of Brad Thorn to the lacerating interventions of Israel Dagg. New Zealand were not found wanting in any phase of the game, bar, perhaps, goal-kicking. Long before the final whistle, the capacity crowd were chanting 'Four More Years', a taunt first used by Wallaby George Gregan when Australia were on their way to a final after defeating the All Blacks in 2003. Revenge was sweet. The scoreboard could have been even more unflattering to Australia, with New Zealand having missed 14 points through kicks.

Everything else was polished. It was no surprise that the All Blacks had scored a try within six minutes of the start. Inevitably Dagg was involved, the coltish New Zealand full back whose speed and angles of running caused so many problems. Dagg flowed on to the ball after a powerful thrust by the forward pack, arcing outside, fending off Wallaby back-row forward Rocky Elsom with ease, and looking for all the world as if he were going to make it to the try line himself. One last despairing tackle by Cooper managed to stem his momentum and looked as if it might have thwarted the move as Dagg toppled towards touch. But he wasn't finished yet. As he fell he managed to pass the ball inside, not with a

desperate fling but with a beautifully weighted float straight into the hands of the supporting Ma'a Nonu, who took grateful receipt and finished things off.

It was a sensational start and boded ill for the Wallabies. They looked as if they were about to be swept away. But,

as they had shown in their rearguard quarter-final victory over the Springboks in Wellington, they know how to put bodies on the line in defence. They certainly had to do so again, with flanker David Pocock once more to the fore, with sterling support from the likes of hooker Stephen Moore and centre Pat McCabe. But it was a forlorn pursuit, an exercise in damage limitation. In a way, Australia were successful, for the scoreline doesn't look as damning as it might have done. The Wallabies were theoretically within touching distance for much of the game, although in truth they were a distant second.

They gave their supporters the occasional frisson of excitement, usually when Digby Ioane got the ball. The Wallaby wing was the lone threat, thrusting through tackles with a strong-hipped shrug and causing the All Blacks to scramble hard themselves in defence. Ioane came so close to nicking one back for Australia shortly after Nonu had touched down. Ioane was headed for the try line until he was grasped and stopped almost in mid-lunge for the whitewash by All Black flanker Jerome Kaino, who somehow managed to wrap his arms around the wing and haul him backwards. It was a

significant moment. A try then might have stemmed the flow and caused a shiver of doubt in All Black minds and given a boost to the Wallabies. But, as was said in many quarters afterwards, this was the All Blacks at their ruthless best. Defence, as much as attack, defines this New Zealand side, who are resolute and unyielding when they need to be. They were decisive in all aspects.

Cooper, in particular, was given the hurry-up by New Zealand, targeted by their kicks and rattled with several bone-crunching follow-up tackles. It was not his finest evening, the

FACING PAGE Live-wire Wallaby wing Digby Ioane gets away from Sam Whitelock and heads for the line, only to be hauled back by Jerome Kaino with the whitewash beneath him. **BELOW** Conrad Smith and helper knock over Wallaby stand-off Quade Cooper. **PAGES 142-143** James O'Connor feels the force of All Black full back Israel Dagg as David Pocock tries to reel him in from behind.

last piece of action seeing him shovelled into touch by his one-time primary-school classmate Richard Kahui.

New Zealand's aerial and kicking game was assured and commanding, with wing Cory Jane time and again rising imperiously to take the ball. Defence is a multi-layered activity. It's not just about smashing your opposite number to kingdom come, although that approach does have its merits; it's also about strategy and precision. Cooper is frail defensively, so he often drops out of the front line. That didn't escape the attention of the All Blacks, who bombarded him with kicks, accompanied by cavalry in the form of wings Jane and Kahui. There was no hiding place. Similarly, they targeted another pivotal Wallaby player, open-side David Pocock, the scourge of the Springboks in the quarter-final. Instead of keeping clear of his larcenous hands, the All Blacks went straight at him, running at him to draw him into the first tackle rather than allowing him to leech at the breakdown.

There was not a phase in which New Zealand were bested. Their scrum became ever stronger, with several powerful shunts earning penalties or disrupting the flow of ball for the Wallabies. No. 8 Kieran Read grew in stature after

■■■ FACING PAGE Rookie fly half Aaron Cruden drops a goal as he settles quickly into the All Black No. 10 berth. BELOW 'Richie McCaw was, well, Richie McCaw – huge-hearted, irrepressible …'

a faltering outing in the quarter-final against Argentina. Second-row Brad Thorn was indestructible despite his advancing years, while Richie McCaw was, well, Richie McCaw – huge-hearted, irrepressible and a hands-down winner in his battle against Pocock. We may have begun to wonder if there was a passing of an era to note, with the All Black skipper a fading force. Those notices are premature. McCaw also had the benefit of a dominant pack to work behind, as he was the first to admit.

If there was one element of the evening which suggested that omissions of previous years have been corrected, it came when young fly half Aaron Cruden popped over a dropped goal midway through the first half. The three points were acclaimed as if the Webb Ellis pot had been placed in the Eden Park trophy cabinet. If the All Blacks had had a similarly pragmatic attitude four years ago in Cardiff, then they might not have lost to France. Every little matters, every point counts this time around.

New Zealand never did quite manage to get clear on the scoreboard, but the outcome, sealed with Piri Weepu's fourth

▬▬ **Full time. The Tri-Nations champions have gone down to a ruthless All Blacks outfit, who now face France in the final.**

penalty goal of the evening in the 72nd minute which brought the score to 20-6, was never in doubt. There was a late yellow card for Sonny Bill Williams, who had only just come onto the field, for a reckless shoulder charge on Cooper, but that was one of the few blemishes on an exhilarating evening.

The All Blacks were determined not to get too far ahead of themselves. 'The job's not yet done,' said Graham Henry. 'It's important we enjoy this moment but then come right back down to earth.'

Well, if Henry wasn't going to suggest that New Zealand were odds-on favourites after this display, then there were plenty of others who were prepared to say it on their behalf, including Wallaby coach Robbie Deans. 'The intent is there with the All Blacks, they're an experienced group, they're well-versed and they're hungry,' said Deans, passed over for the All Black coaching job four years ago as Graham Henry was retained. 'They'll take a lot of stopping from here.'

This had been Australia's heaviest ever defeat in a World Cup match. On its own, that was a stunning statistic, a measure of the quality of the opposition. Yet the All Blacks had brushed them aside with barely a backward glance. Onwards they went.

Jerome Kaino picks up wing Digby Ioane and hauls him back from the line to save a Wallaby score.

SEMI-FINAL
BLACK BLITZ
What they said...

New Zealand: Graham Henry (coach)

The team had a huge physical presence from minute one to minute 80. The boys were heroic and their character was superb and you can't ask for more than that. Everyone who took the field gave 100 per cent. The defence was quite outstanding. It's a good feeling.

New Zealand: Richie McCaw (captain)

Every man did his bit. That's what you have to do in World Cup rugby. I'm very happy with that. I thought our back three were outstanding. The kickers put the ball in front of us at the right times. It makes it easy for forwards. The intensity, the ball carriers and the breakdown were the key. Israel Dagg from the back was outstanding.

New Zealand: Cory Jane (wing)

My job is to catch the high ball. I have to catch them and if I don't I shouldn't be in this team.

New Zealand: Piri Weepu (scrum half)

I guess it's a stepping stone to where I want to be and I'm grateful for the opportunity. It's a great achievement for me after coming off last week and getting the bad news about the death of my grandfather. I'm pretty sure he's looking down on me and is very proud.

New Zealand: Aaron Cruden (fly half), a late addition to the squad

It has been a pretty surreal couple of weeks – extraordinary and emotional. It was great to get the late call-up ahead of a World Cup semi-final.

Australia: Robbie Deans (coach)

Their work in the air was superior to ours. They secured the ball in the air where we didn't. When they kicked they were able to apply more pressure.

on the mercurial Quade Cooper

There's two ways he can go – absorb it, but maintain focus on things that are important. Or turn your toes up. I'd like to think he won't be doing the latter.

It's easy to take a potshot. I think the way he's carried himself has been impressive. His errors are a sideshow.

Australia: James Horwill (captain)

It's really disappointing to finish like that. They did very well in the air. They outplayed us and deserved to win. The All Blacks are a great side. We hung in there, but they ticked the scoreboard over in the second half. They defended very well. We didn't execute and put phases together. We didn't pressure at their end of the field.

Australia: James O'Connor (wing)

They beat us in every facet. They used the ball well and the physicality was right up there. Everything went their way and we couldn't do anything about it. It's tough when you are starved of all the ball. They were clinical and we've never met physicality like that before.

Australia: Dan Vickerman (lock)

The group is pretty low. We played in our half, which is not the best thing to do in a World Cup semi-final. We didn't play the way we wanted and came off second-best.

Australia: Quade Cooper (fly half)

I am who I am. I'm going to play the way I do. Whether you like it or not – that's me.

Fly half Quade Cooper slots a dropped goal for the Wallabies.

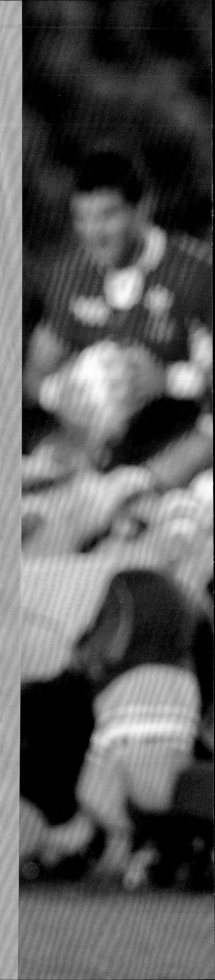

RUGBY
WORLD CUP
2011

AUCKLAND

New Zealand 2011

BRONZE FINAL
THE WALLABIES PREVAIL
IAN ROBERTSON

Wales **18** | **21** Australia

The endless controversy over the red card for Sam Warburton dragged on right through the week leading up to the third-place play-off game and overshadowed the build-up.

This was a great shame because the Welsh team reduced to 14 players for the last hour of their semi-final against France played quite magnificently. The blunt truth is Wales deserved to win and indeed should have won. The most damaging statistic is not necessarily the sending-off of Warburton but the fact that Wales missed six kicks at goal and yet only lost by one point. Almost all of those kicks were eminently kickable. Two were dropped goals in front of the posts, along with three penalties from relatively easy angles. The most difficult was the conversion of Mike Phillips' try, but Stephen Jones missed a kick he would have nailed 19 times out of 20.

All of this doubtless preyed on the minds of the Welsh squad during the final week of the tournament and it must inevitably have had a detrimental and negative effect. It took until the eve of the match against Australia before the Welsh camp conceded that the change in the law on the dangerous tackle which was made in December 2010, only nine months before the start of the World Cup, actually left referee Alain Rolland no option whatever but to give Warburton a red card.

The change in the law states that if a player tips an opponent up so that that player's legs are off the ground up in the air and he then lets go so the player crashes to the ground under his own steam, it is still an automatic red card. Previously the referee could use his discretion and have the option of giving a yellow card, but that option was taken away in December 2010.

The fact remains that it was a very harsh decision, but strictly according to the letter of the law it was the correct

Australia's No. 8 Ben McCalman puts his side 21-11 up with just four minutes left to play.

decision. Of course, it changed the whole game. Of course, the Welsh felt very hard done by and of course the whole rugby world felt total sympathy with the awful predicament the Welsh found themselves in.

What was quite remarkable was the resilience they showed in adversity to keep themselves in the match right up to the final whistle. If only they could have kicked just one of their six shots at goal.

I have brought this whole episode up because there is no question it left its mark on the team as they prepared for the bronze-medal match. They talked of the empty feeling they were all experiencing as they began training for a match they felt they should not be playing. Wales should have been in the final and not the third-place play-off match.

Worse still, they would have to go into their last World Cup game with three key players missing. Sam Warburton was suspended for his dangerous tackle and they were also without Rhys Priestland and Adam Jones.

Priestland had had a tremendous campaign both as a fly half and even more importantly, as it transpired, as a goal-kicker. He was hugely missed against Australia. So too was Jones. He was a crucial figure in the Welsh scrum and they were not nearly as effective without him.

History has shown that the play-off match is often an anticlimax. For Wales in Auckland this was certainly the case. They had played so well throughout the whole tournament that it must have been really disappointing that they slipped at the final hurdle.

A crowd of 53,000 turned up at Eden Park and they witnessed a game in which Australia always had the edge. The Wallabies had a rare experience when they were able to boast the better scrummage. This gave them a platform they had not enjoyed against New Zealand in the semi-finals. They also had the better of the line out, which might have been different if Sam Warburton had been playing.

For the first time in six weeks Quade Cooper looked the part at fly half and Australia dominated the territory and the possession. Berrick Barnes took full advantage of a half-gap created by Cooper to slice through and score by the posts. James O'Connor converted for a 7-0 lead after 11 minutes. The only other score in the first half came midway through, when James Hook landed a penalty. It was 7-3 to Australia at half-time.

Wales stuck to the task and were rewarded with a blistering try by Shane Williams. After all the bad luck Wales

Shane Williams collects his kick-ahead and dives over for his fifty-seventh try for Wales to give them a slender 8-7 lead with half an hour to run on the clock.

had had recently, they had a stroke of good fortune when the pass to Williams looked decidedly forward, but referee Wayne Barnes has a habit of missing forward passes at World Cups and Wales benefited. Williams lurched forward to kick the ball through and, at the end of a great kick and chase, the Welsh Wizard scored his fifty-seventh try for his country. The conversion was missed. The score was 8-7 to Wales with 30 minutes left.

In the next seven minutes James O'Connor kicked two penalties in quick succession to put Australia back in front 13-8. With 13 minutes left, the Wallabies virtually sealed the match with a dropped goal from Berrick Barnes, who had played with great confidence, first at centre, then at fly half after he moved inside to replace Quade Cooper when the latter injured a knee in the first half.

A glimmer of hope surfaced for Wales in the 70th minute when Stephen Jones kicked a penalty to cut the deficit to

FACING PAGE, TOP Berrick Barnes kicks a 67th-minute dropped goal to extend Australia's lead to eight points. Barnes had moved to fly half after a serious knee injury to Quade Cooper. **LEFT** George North and Leigh Halfpenny dispossess Adam Ashley-Cooper with the line at the Wallaby's mercy. **ABOVE** Leigh Halfpenny runs in to cap with a try a remarkable final passage of play by Wales.

153

16-11. With four minutes left that hope was ended. Ben McCalman scored Australia's second try from broken play to leave the Wallabies with a comfortable 21-11 lead.

What followed was a truly amazing end to the match.

There was no time left for Wales to score twice. But, unbelievably, there was time for them to score once and score one of the best tries of this and any other World Cup.

With one minute left they had a scrum five metres from their own line. They won the scrum and began to make their way 100 metres to the Australian line. It was a quite phenomenal effort. It took them over three minutes and they won 30 rucks and mauls in the process. The concentration, discipline and determination were outstanding. The coup de grâce came way into added time, with Leigh Halfpenny scoring the second Welsh try. Stephen Jones converted.

The Wallabies won the match and the bronze medal. The Welsh won the hearts of a nation and they can be very proud of their 2011 World Cup campaign. They came so close to glory.

ABOVE Wales take their leave of Eden Park and the 2011 World Cup, in which they made many friends and admirers with their brand of rugby. **LEFT** A memorable evening for Nathan Sharpe, who won a World Cup bronze medal but also his 100th Wallaby cap.

Wallabies coach Robbie Deans with his players after victory in the bronze final at Eden Park.

2011

BRONZE FINAL
THE WALLABIES PREVAIL
What they said...

Australia: Robbie Deans (coach)

This match is not easy because players are disappointed at being knocked out. It's still an opportunity to represent your country. We came to win the tournament, but were not good enough by some distance.

Australia: James Horwill (captain)

We had to be strong at the breakdown and David Pocock got key steals. Losing Quade and Kurtley made it tough. We adapted well and wanted to show a bit of rugby. We made the most of a situation we didn't want to be in. We made Nathan Sharpe's night memorable.

Australia: Will Genia (scrum half) on Quade Cooper

He showed a lot of guts and he'll be much better for it. The applause when he left was a change from all the booing.

Australia: Digby Ioane (wing)

People hate Quade because they can't do what he does. He is representing Australia and New Zealand. I do not understand why he gets a bad reception.

Australia: James O'Connor (wing)

With Quade and Kurtley off early, it was a good opportunity for me to step up to that ball-playing role.

on the subject of the match balls

They were never a problem. They've got a sweet spot.

Wales: Warren Gatland (coach)

We were not emotionally up for it. Wales learned a massive amount from seven Tests. They've been through a lot and will be stronger.

Wales: Shaun Edwards (defence coach)

The youngsters emerged only because Warren had the guts to select them and also trust the subs. People criticised Rhys Priestland's selection. They must be watching a different game. An inspired choice.

Wales: Gethin Jenkins (captain)

We enjoyed the tournament but it was a shame we couldn't finish with a win instead of a close defeat. To get to the semis is a great achievement and to come fourth is still an improvement on some World Cups.

Wales: Ryan Jones (No. 8)

We thought we could do something special. We really wanted a medal. We put Wales back on the rugby map. Some guys played the best rugby of their careers.

Wales: Shane Williams (wing)

The spirit and atmosphere throughout the camp has been fantastic. We can achieve a lot as we have some great youngsters.

Wales: Mike Phillips (scrum half)

Shane Williams is a genius who makes magic happen – the sort of player that fans want to see.

Wales: Jamie Roberts (centre)

To lose to South Africa and France by a point, and Australia by three, shows the fine lines at this level. If we get things right, we'll put those teams away. We haven't beaten a southern hemisphere team here.

Wales's Andy Powell looks for a way through the Wallabies.

FINAL
BLACKS HOLD THEIR NERVE
JOHN INVERDALE

France **7** | **8** New Zealand

Colonel Gaddafi was killed three days before the final of the Rugby World Cup. A not insignificant event, you might think, on the global stage.

Yet it was of considerably less import to the people of New Zealand than 22 men in black attempting to fulfil a nation's sporting destiny. In fact on the day after the Libyan tyrant's demise, it was only on page 22 of its news section that *The New Zealand Herald* got round to discussing the issue, although not perhaps in the manner that most international visitors might expect: 'Gaddafi's dead? Yawn. What time's the final?'

By the day of the match, it was all about 'immortality' awaiting the soon-to-be-victorious All Blacks, pre-christened the 'Unshakeables' in an oblique reference to the Christchurch earthquake.

But if the media coverage in advance of the game was suffocating, rarely can a major city by the sea have been so claustrophobic. To walk along the waterfront was to be engulfed in a human oil slick of black jerseys. Never can the

culmination of an international sporting event have been so lacking in colour. It was just all black. All black and more black. And the great thing of course was that all the ABs had to do was turn up, demolish the last remains of the French rabble who had somehow made it into the final, and Richie McCaw would duly lift the World Cup, putting an end to 24 years of being 'chokers'.

In the radio area at Eden Park, not a single French commentator thought their side had a chance. By common consent, this was the worst team ever to reach a final. One predicted a French triumph 17-12 and then erupted in a Clouseau-esque bout of hysterical laughter.

BUT … both we and they were overlooking one thing. This was the French we were talking about. The maddening, infuriating French who always have one great game in them at every World Cup.

And they meant business. As the All Blacks lined up for the haka, the French formed an arrowhead formation, with the indomitable Thierry Dusautoir at the front, and then as Piri Weepu reached explosion point and Ali Williams' tongue

■ **The 24-year wait is over. The All Blacks are world champions once again.**

(surely the longest in international rugby) almost crossed the halfway line, the French fanned out and marched towards the New Zealanders. A moment of sporting theatre but also a clear declaration of intent.

There then followed a magical rugby occasion. A match of such intensity and tension that it took the breath away. The early French storm blew itself out, and soon Les Bleus (playing in white) were tackling for all they were worth. Weepu, the cult hero of the tournament once Dan Carter had been injured, missed a penalty, and then a conversion after the unlikely figure of Tony Woodcock scored a try from a line out when the French defence parted alarmingly. That was surely the precursor to an avalanche of New Zealand scores as the team who had lost to Tonga capitulated ignominiously.

Except 5-0 was the half-time score. A nasty cheap shot on Morgan Parra had forced him from the field, but it was a piece of skulduggery that backfired on the Blacks. Enter François Trinh-Duc to start playing like outside halves are supposed to – astute tactical kicking, the occasional coruscating half-break and one surging run that might have brought a try but for a desperate tap tackle.

And in a bizarre twist, the All Blacks also had a new No. 10 just before the break. Aaron Cruden, the replacement for the replacement, turned a knee, and onto the biggest stage of all came Stephen Donald, the replacement for the replacement for the replacement, who two weeks earlier had

been fishing for whitebait, hanging on the line waiting for a call from AB management saying 'your country needs you'.

Well, it did. In the very first minute of the second half, a penalty opportunity 40 metres out in front of the posts. Donald struck it perfectly and the score was 8-0. Nerves calmed. The Rolling Stones' 'Paint It Black' blared out. It's all over now. Except the French would not fade away. In fact they got stronger. The back-row trio of Bonnaire, Harinordoquy and Dusautoir rampaged, tackled, caught line-out balls and then did some more rampaging. Yachvili pulled the strings, and Trinh-Duc fed Rougerie constantly as the buccaneering centre bashed and smashed his way at and through Nonu and Smith in the All Black midfield. A New Zealand journalist remarked that it was like watching a Six Nations international as opposed to a Tri-Nations basketball

LEFT Not going quietly. Skipper Thierry Dusautoir leads his men towards the New Zealand haka ahead of the game. **FACING PAGE, BELOW** Morgan Parra brings down Ma'a Nonu early in the game. A blow to the head soon forced the French fly half off, to be replaced by François Trinh-Duc. **BELOW** Tony Woodcock opens the scoring for the All Blacks after a quarter of an hour.

game. And it was all the better for that. The French captain went over by the posts, and the conversion narrowed the margin to a single point with half an hour to go. This was surely not going to be the upset to end all upsets?

Nothing happened and everything happened in that final half-hour. Each and every player on both sides knew an

infringement here and a penalty there might be the difference between victory and defeat. Referee Craig Joubert was subsequently accused of abdicating his reponsibilities when McCaw especially went offside at a ruck, but it would have been a brave man who gave France a shot at goal with time running out. The French tried desperately to manoeuvre themselves into dropped-goal territory, but the All Black defence was supreme. It was so tense you had to remind yourself to breathe.

And then with four minutes to go, the All Blacks won a penalty and began to run the clock down. For 76 minutes it had been breathless and helter-skelter, and then it died. Pick and drive, pick and drive, tick, tick, tick. Isn't that the kind of rugby the New Zealanders despise? Not tonight. They applauded every yard gained, every second spent, as if Israel Dagg had run half the length to score.

Dimitri Szarzewski got fed up and impetuously went offside. A kickable penalty, but nobody cared. Eighty minutes was up; 4.4 million people could breathe easy. The orang-utan on a nation's back had been shaken off. New Zealand may not have been the best on the day, but it mattered not.

███ **FACING PAGE** Replacement All Black fly half Stephen Donald prepares to launch what proved to be the winning kick. **RIGHT** Piri Weepu's flying tap tackle stops François Trinh-Duc. **BELOW** Hard-running centre Aurélien Rougerie finds himself the focus of All Black attention. **PAGES 162-163** Kieran Read on the rampage.

FINAL *BLACKS HOLD THEIR NERVE*

The All Blacks were where they belonged – at the top of the international rugby tree.

A few statistics to share with you. France had 55 per cent of territory and possession. The All Blacks made 24 more tackles repelling the waves of attacks in the second half. A jaundiced French journalist mused that his nation had managed to squeeze past 14 men in the semi-final but found playing 16 in the final beyond them. It remains one of the weaknesses of the game that so often the most significant figure on the field is the man with the whistle, but until the laws change, it will forever remain that way. Had Trinh-Duc been successful with a penalty attempt from near halfway, the French would have pulled off the biggest shock in sport since Buster Douglas beat Mike Tyson. But he didn't and they didn't, and it was probably the right result. New Zealand had been the best team in the tournament, and the best team in the world for the past four years. No team in history had ever won a World Cup having lost a match in the tournament, and the French had lost two. But on the final whistle their pride had been more than restored, and we had at least seen one team wearing white in New Zealand who merited a standing ovation. Dusautoir's performance even exceeded Pocock's for Australia against South Africa, and a mark of the man's

LEFT Israel Dagg and Damien Traille give no quarter over a high ball. **FACING PAGE** Thierry Dusautoir cuts through by the posts to score for France. **BELOW** Pascal Papé of France has replacement All Black scrum half Andy Ellis in his sights. **PAGES 166-167** At last … At last. Richie McCaw lifts the Webb Ellis Cup at Eden Park.

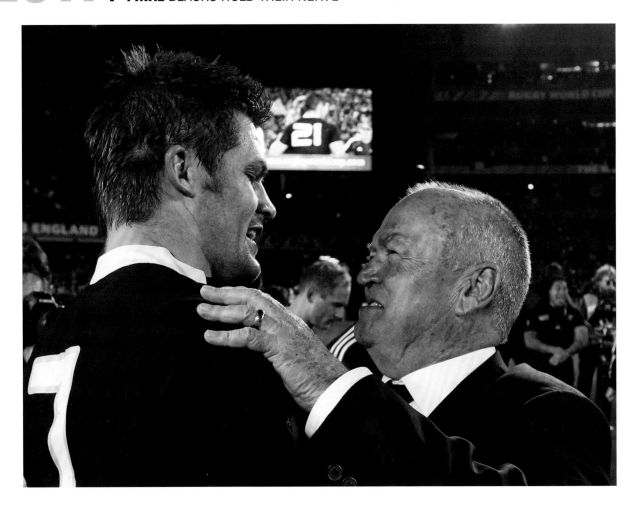

■ Captain Richie McCaw and coach Graham Henry celebrate the fruits of many years of labour.

quality was that nearly two hours after the final whistle, he was on the touch line going through an extensive debrief on the match for French television.

And what of Marc Lièvremont? you ask. Pass. He cut a forlorn figure at the end, walking round alone, making minimal contact with his players. Or should that be ex-players? He'd lost them long since. What really did happen in the preceding weeks? His autobiography will be one sporting book well worth the wait.

But history is written by the victors, so mention must be made of Thorn and Read, who were immense in the All Black pack, and the fact that when a golden opportunity presented itself for the ABs to choke under almost unbearable pressure, they didn't. McCaw was a genuinely great leader, and Graham Henry, laconic and dry throughout the campaign, permitted himself the broadest of smiles because his

meticulous planning had come good in the end. He'd added pragmatism to the All Blacks' list of qualities, and that more than anything was what they needed on the night.

I am writing this in a coffee bar on Auckland waterfront the morning after the night before. A cruise ship is just leaving port with barely a single porthole not displaying an All Black flag. The clean-up operation after the mother of all-nighters is in full swing. The streets are initially surprisingly busy until you realise that a lot of people haven't gone to bed yet. By some fortuitous twist of fate, today is a national holiday. Now that is what you call planning.

And *The New Zealand Herald*? The front page sums up what it all means. 'After a shocking 12 months for our country – more than 200 killed in the Christchurch earthquake and at the Pike River mine – the victory stretches far beyond the rugby field. It's a triumph for the nation, and the dawn of a new legacy of All Black dominance.'

In a land far, far away, they will sleep easy. As world champions.

The moment of glory.

FINAL
BLACKS HOLD THEIR NERVE

What they said...

New Zealand: Graham Henry (coach)

To win means everything. We showed that All Blacks tenacity. Stephen Donald came on and played bloody well. He kicked what turned out to be the winning goal and gave us field position. I knew he could handle it. I was nervous the whole game.

We've been the top team in the world for a long time. I have so much respect for Richie and the boys, hanging in there right through the 80 minutes to win this thing, and for what they've done over eight years.

New Zealand: Richie McCaw (captain)

We had to dig deeper than ever. We couldn't have been under more pressure. It was 30 guys, the management and everyone played their part. Around New Zealand people supported us so much and it's great that we could repay them. There's going to be a lot of stories told as we get older. We left everything out there.

New Zealand: Tony Woodcock (prop) on his try and other matters

It's unbelievable. We had to fight for it. It just opened up. It was pretty satisfying to have that move up our sleeve. It was definitely a team effort. The last 20 minutes we just defended and defended and throughout I thought of 2007. A lot of guys won't be involved again, so it's good to have that under the belt. Richie does everything for the team.

New Zealand: Jerome Kaino (flanker)

Seeing Richie and Keven Mealamu lift that trophy is an awesome feeling, but we didn't expect anything less.

New Zealand: Stephen Donald (fly half)

I'm fortunate to get the opportunity to come into a great team – to get the chance to prove that I am an All Black is good.

All Blacks Nonu, Williams, Kaino, Donald and Kahui share a joke on the winners' rostrum.

FINAL BLACKS HOLD THEIR NERVE

New Zealand: Piri Weepu (scrum half)

■ *The French came out to play and showed what they were capable of. These are moments that I will remember for the rest of my life.*

New Zealand: Keven Mealamu (hooker)

■ *I feel a lot of relief. I haven't slept well for the last couple of months. I'll sleep well tonight.*

France: Marc Lièvremont (coach)

■ *It is tremendously sad. I met referee Craig Joubert two days ago and told him he was the best. I told him there was tremendous pressure in the final game and a man sometimes makes mistakes. I will not criticise him.*

■ *The squad made many promises to themselves and they kept them. The second half was one-way traffic. We made the All Blacks tremble. I thought the performance of my players was beautiful. It is hard when you are up against a whole nation.*

■ *My contract ends today [the day after the final]. I know some players were not happy with me. I have great admiration for them and I hope in the coming weeks they will feel the same way about me. I have all good memories.*

France: Thierry Dusautoir (captain)

■ *It's a real pity. I am proud of what my boys did in the World Cup. We lost two games in the pool and we came to the final. I do not criticise referees. Tonight there was lots of time left at 8-7, but we did not do enough to get that vital penalty. But we could not do more. Maybe we needed more skill. Tonight everyone was nervous – all 30 players were scared.*

■ *At one point in the haka we were so close that they wanted to kiss the New Zealanders.*

France: Dimitri Yachvili (scrum half)

■ *We thought that we must give everything so that we would not have any regrets.*

France: Maxime Mermoz (centre)

■ *Everything that was said about us was motivation.*

France: Julien Bonnaire (flanker)

■ *We come out of the competition with our head up. To lose by one point! It's so cruel! This World Cup was a roller coaster and somehow we are happy to leave the competition this way. We showed that France deserved their final.*

LEFT Keven Mealamu (second left) deep in conversation with Mils Muliaina (in suit). **ABOVE** Marc Lièvremont casts a wistful glance at the Webb Ellis Cup.

LOOKING BACK
SPIRIT OF NEW ZEALAND
CHRIS HEWETT

So it was that the Stadium of Four Million, as promised by the New Zealand hosts, came to pass.

Indeed, in the hours before the final between the All Blacks and France, it seemed as though at least three million of those folk were in Auckland – either packed into the supporters' zones on the waterfront or thronging the 'fan trail' that started a few metres from the harbour and ended at Eden Park. As a symbol of the success of this seventh World Cup, it could not have been bettered.

New Zealanders of every stripe will think of the competition as a triumph every time they look at the record book and set eyes on the unlikely climactic scoreline: 8-7 to their men – an old-fashioned 15-point thriller if ever there was one. But there was more to getting it right than having the most accomplished all-round side in the draw prevailing at the death over the most dangerous. Success demanded something else, something beyond home-town ecstasy.

Here was a tournament to capture the mind and spirit: pretty much from the get-go, there was rugby of a vibrant, challenging kind. Had anyone imagined that Romania would be leading Scotland late in the game; or that Japan would scare the pants off Les Bleus; or that the United States would be so competitive against Ireland; or that Wales would dominate the Springboks, both physically and territorially, before losing to the reigning champions by a point? Of course not. Yet all this happened on the first weekend, and there would be further fun and games as the pool stage unfolded.

The one blight on the competition was a fixture schedule hopelessly loaded in favour of the major nations – a programme driven by broadcasters with one eye on the mass viewing market back in Europe. Namibia, one of the two weakest sides, really copped it: their matches with the hard-hitting South Sea islanders of Fiji and Samoa were separated by 96 hours, and later in the phase, they played the Boks on

Maxime Médard is caught by Alisi Tupuailai as France are given a scare by Japan at the North Harbour Stadium.

Captain of Namibia Jacques Burger charges Samoa's Anthony Perenise in Rotorua. Burger, one of the tournament's outstanding performers, plays his club rugby for Saracens in England.

a Thursday night before meeting the in-form Welsh the following Monday. Did anyone die of shock when the gaps between the professional sides and the amateurs widened as the tournament moved into its third and fourth weeks? Apparently not.

Yet the so-called 'minnows' still made their mark. Assessed strictly in context, there were no better loose forwards in the whole event than Jacques Burger of Namibia and Mamuka Gorgodze of Georgia; no more combative hooker than Marius Tincu of Romania; no more dangerous wide runner than Vasily Artemyev of Russia. Once the totals in the 'points against' columns started to pile up – the direct result of coaches withholding their best players from contests with the Tier One countries so they would be fresh for games in which victory was a possibility – the criticism of the 20-team format began to mount. Those critics might, however, care to remember that across the opening two rounds of matches, the winning margins between the privileged foundation nations and the rest were lower on average than at any point since 1991.

There was also much to admire in the rugby of the usual suspects from outside the 'big eight'. With a little luck, Samoa would have made the last four: certainly, they looked good enough to do so when their coach, Titimaea Tafua, picked the right side, with David Lemi and Eliota Fuimaono-Sapolu

(tweeter extraordinaire, and no mean centre either) in the back division. Argentina? Phenomenally resourceful and good value for their place in the last eight. Tonga? Terrific, after a sloppy first half against the hosts on opening night and a bargain-basement performance against Canada.

Flipsides? England, of course: poor on the pitch, worse off it. Fiji were a disappointment too – the palest imaginable shadow of the 2007 vintage. But those are small quibbles, because the overall experience provided by the most vibrant rugby community on earth made form an irrelevance. Every restaurant, every bar, every corner shop – rugby conversation was everywhere and there was no escaping it. Or any desire to escape it. So the teenage girl selling you a dollar's worth of chewing gum thought the English midfield was rubbish? Great. Why not? Her opinion was as good as anyone's.

There will be bigger World Cups, financially speaking. There may even be better ones in a rugby sense – tournaments with two or three genuinely great sides, as opposed to none. But there will never be another one quite like this, because the special spirit of the All Black nation cannot be replicated.

LOOKING AHEAD
RUGBY IN THE SPOTLIGHT
IAN ROBERTSON

After seven World Cups have produced two ultimate triumphs each for New Zealand, Australia and South Africa, and one for England, it is worth looking ahead to see if anything is likely to alter.

Of course, the three Tri-Nations teams will continue to be a major force, with England and France lurking ominously in the background. But it just may be that times are changing. Thanks to the generous sponsorship of HSBC, the International Rugby Board World Sevens circuit is making a major impact in the world game. It is spreading the gospel of rugby far afield and capturing a new audience.

In 2012, the HSBC Sevens World Series will be played in nine countries – New Zealand, South Africa, Australia, Japan, Hong Kong, USA, Dubai, England and Scotland. This fascinating rugby circuit began in humble surroundings but has developed quickly and has rapidly caught the imagination of a wider public. Sevens rugby is fast, exciting

and very much easier for spectators to follow than the 15-a-side game.

The HSBC Hong Kong Sevens in 2012 will be the core event of the whole series, with the biggest, most interactive audience, and this tournament's pre-eminence dates back to the early 1980s when, it seemed, the whole rugby world decamped every year to Hong Kong at the end of March.

As the popularity of Sevens has grown worldwide, a major landmark was reached in 2009 when the four-yearly World Cup for Sevens was held in Dubai. It was watched and analysed by two members of the International Olympic Committee (IOC). They reported back to the IOC that Rugby Sevens was an ideal event for the Olympic Games. It was a great spectacle and played by both men and women. Rugby had last appeared at the Olympics in 1924, when the USA collected the gold medal.

To the delight of the rugby world, the Olympic Committee voted to include Rugby Sevens in the 2016

JJ Gagiano of the USA scores against Australia. The inclusion of Sevens in the Olympics could mean big things for American rugby.

Supporting the growth of world rugby.

At HSBC, we're committed to the growth of rugby across the globe. We understand that the game has the capacity to connect different people, cultures and communities. Our investment in the sport spans from grass roots rugby right through to the highest level of the professional game. Which is why we are proud sponsors of the HSBC Asian Five Nations, the HSBC Sevens World Series, the HSBC Penguin International Coaching Academy and the British and Irish Lions Tour to Australia in 2013.

The world's local bank

Issued by HSBC Holdings plc.

Olympic Games in Rio de Janeiro. This is a huge boost for the game of rugby and has widespread implications. A great number of countries' teams, most notably that of the USA, the defending Olympic champions, will receive significant financial support from their respective governments simply because rugby has become an Olympic sport. There is huge potential for several second-tier countries to improve dramatically with a large injection of cash to help the development of the game.

Rugby in America, for example, will suddenly have the financial clout to attract a whole raft of talented American footballers who have narrowly failed to land lucrative contracts with the Chicago Bears or the Dallas Cowboys but could become outstanding rugby union players and at the same time earn considerable sums of money pursuing a new career in an Olympic sport. Fiji, Samoa and Tonga will have a new shop window to parade their talents in Rio de Janeiro in 2016. The Rugby World Cup has a big global television audience – the Olympic Games has a vastly bigger one.

The inclusion of Sevens in the Olympics will mean that rugby is to be a major highlight and a focus of attention three years in a row. In 2015 there will be the Rugby World Cup in England; in 2016 Rugby Sevens will be a feature of the Olympic Games in Brazil; and in 2017 the Lions will tour New Zealand. This is a massive opportunity for rugby to showcase the sport. As an appetizer, the sixth Rugby World Cup Sevens takes place in Russia in 2013. At the time of writing the

Tonga's scrum half Taniela Moa escapes the clutches of Richie McCaw during RWC 2011's opening match at Eden Park. The Sevens in Rio will give the Tongans and other South Sea islanders another chance to strut their stuff on the world stage.

tournament has been scheduled for June, at exactly the same time as the Lions Test series in Australia. This is an unbelievable clash; as HSBC sponsor the Lions as well as the Sevens circuit, one can only pray this can be sorted out. The hope is that the IRB see the folly of their ways and reschedule the Sevens two or three months earlier.

Rugby is in a strong position and must take full advantage of every opportunity it has to develop its appeal.

What is encouraging is that the 2015 World Cup in England looks guaranteed to be a great success. Just under 1.4 million spectators turned up at the grounds to watch the 48 matches in New Zealand in 2011. More than double that number are expected to watch the 2015 tournament. It is destined to be the most successful World Cup ever. Rugby at both 15-a-side and seven-a-side is in a very healthy state.

In 2011 the IRB was delighted to announce that the board had signed a five-year sponsorship deal with HSBC to secure the future of the Sevens circuit. It has increased the series from eight tournaments to nine, with Japan becoming the new venue.

For Sevens as well as Fifteens, it is onwards and upwards.

OFFICIAL WATCH OF
RUGBY WORLD CUP 2011

1860 Edouard Heuer founded his workshop in the Swiss Jura.
1916 First mechanical stopwatch accurate to 1/100th of a second.
1969 First automatic chronograph.
2011 TAG Heuer CARRERA Calibre 16 Day-Date.

Available at TAG Heuer boutiques and selected fine jewellers nationwide.
For more information visit www.tagheuer.com
TM © Rugby World Cup Limited 2008

TAG HEUER PLAYER OF THE TOURNAMENT

RICHIE McCAW

STEPHEN JONES

Richie McCaw found that a host of contenders were snapping at his heels during the Rugby World Cup.

A man who has been unchallenged as the greatest open-side flanker of his generation was suddenly being hunted in what turned out to be a glorious mini-era in the history of open-side play.

There was David Pocock of Australia, Sam Warburton of Wales, Heinrich Brüssow of South Africa, Maurie Fa'asavalu of Samoa and several others. Because of the way the game is currently played and because an accident of birth transported a group of richly talented men to New Zealand, McCaw no longer had it his own way.

His reaction was almost beyond praise. He may not even have been quite at a blazing career peak because a foot injury which afflicted him almost throughout the tournament reduced a little of his efficiency, and sent New Zealanders into paroxysms of panic. But we are talking here about a gigantic Black package. About a man whose play, example, aura and leadership played a monumental part in New Zealand's triumph.

And also about a man whose magnificence in resistance when France had the ascendancy in the final itself did more than anything to calm the ragged nerves of a team, a stadium and a nation. His anticipation and cunning in those closing stages were remarkable, and in common with any other great flanker, it can be said that he earned the right to play at the very limit of the offside line and the laws themselves.

The reverence for him in the country is pervading. If you travel along New Zealand's Highway 1 along the east coast of the South Island, you encounter Oamaru, where McCaw was born. The sign for Oamaru is dwarfed by another sign which says simply 'Birthplace of Richie McCaw'. It was also during the World Cup pool stage that he won his 100th cap for New

▬▬ **At the heart of things. All Black skipper Richie McCaw prepares to hand off the ball during the final.**

Worth the wait. Richie McCaw with the Webb Ellis Cup after leading New Zealand to a tense 8-7 victory over France in the final.

Zealand, this after a decade in the Black jersey. It was an affecting sight when after the game he was presented with a special white cap to mark the century, by Jock Hobbs, himself a world-class flanker in his time, who was battling serious illness. There were few dry eyes in the house.

Statistics often show very little about the contribution of a player, but McCaw's stats are incredible. He has won almost exactly 90 per cent of the games in which he has played for his country. He has been captain of the All Blacks in almost half of the 103 Tests he has played. He has been the IRB Player of the Year a record three times, and he must have come perilously close on this occasion, with only the almost indescribably brilliant performance of French captain Thierry Dusautoir in the final itself seeing the Frenchman ease ahead.

And it is the sheer longevity and the implacable nature of his warrior spirit which struck you in the tournament. Arguably, he plays in the most physically arduous and even dangerous position on the field, insinuating himself where all kinds of flying boots are apt to connect. These days, predatory flankers of his kind find that opponents actually target them individually, ignoring the ball and making heavy contact as they arrive on the scene. If you can't beat them, smash them.

How remarkable, therefore, that when McCaw actually lifted the Webb Ellis Cup above his head on that emotional night at Eden Park, Auckland, for a moment all the exhaustion and the bruises were lost in a kind of youthful radiance. There is no one on earth who would have begrudged New Zealand that moment, and no one on earth would have dared to challenge the right of Richie McCaw to savour it by the second.

HSBC WORLD XV
THE BEST OF RWC 2011
IAN ROBERTSON

The selection of the 2011 World XV was not quite as straightforward as it should have been. Dan Carter would be the first choice on everybody's team sheet at fly half.

However, a cruel and unexpected injury ruled Carter out of the tournament before the knockout stages began, so a huge gap was left. Carter remains the best fly half in world rugby but all of the World XV played at least one match in the knockout stages and Carter did not.

Full back was a much easier call. Mils Muliaina would have been on every shortlist prior to the start of the World Cup, but the promotion of Israel Dagg changed all that. Dagg improved with every game, and by the final he was accepted as the number one player in that position. Kurtley Beale of Australia and England's Ben Foden played well and so did Maxime Médard of France, but Dagg gets the vote.

New Zealand played well throughout the tournament and were never really stretched until the final, so with their forwards on top in every match, life was relatively easy for the backs. On that basis Ma'a Nonu was outstanding and thoroughly deserves to be in the World XV. Partnering Nonu in the centre, Conrad Smith was perhaps the obvious choice, but preference has been given to Jamie Roberts of Wales. He was tremendous in all the big matches and even though he prefers the No. 12 jersey, it seemed that with a little poetic licence we could accommodate the best two centres in the whole World Cup. On the wings, both Kiwis had really good tournaments, so Cory Jane and Richard Kahui made the shortlist, but they faced serious competition. Five other players had to be factored in to the equation – George North and Shane Williams of Wales, Vincent Clerc of France, along with Digby Ioane and James O'Connor of Australia. A really tough decision, but into the final side go George North on the right wing and Vincent Clerc on the left.

At fly half no obvious candidate emerged after injury ended Dan Carter's campaign, although the odds favoured Aaron Cruden, who had the massive benefit of playing behind the rampant All Blacks pack. Many of the leading fly halves in the quarter-finals ruled themselves out with

▬ **The impressive Rhys Priestland looks to spin the ball against South Africa in Wales's opening game of the 2011 World Cup.**

substandard performances – Quade Cooper, Jonny Wilkinson, James Hook, Ronan O'Gara and Morgan Parra. The best players up to the semi-finals were Rhys Priestland of Wales and Felipe Contepomi of Argentina, although he played mostly at centre. This selection was very difficult.

Aaron Cruden only came in at the knockout stages of the tournament but played well considering his lack of experience at international level. Playing fly half for the All Blacks during the World Cup was not the hardest job in the world, but although he played perfectly well he did not quite have the X-factor, and so controversially the selection at No. 10 is Felipe Contepomi. He masterminded the brave Argentine effort throughout their campaign and was unquestionably their star back. He is equally at home at centre or fly half, and we think he would be very comfortable in our World XV in the latter position.

At scrum half the selection was very close between Mike Phillips of Wales, Dimitri Yachvili of France and Will Genia of Australia. Piri Weepu falls short of being a great scrum half because his service to his fly half is not as quick or as good as the passes possessed by the above shortlist of three. In a close vote, Phillips was chosen.

In the pack, the really hard decisions came in the back row, where so many teams had outstanding players. At No. 8, Sergio Parisse was phenomenal for Italy, but because his team failed to reach the knockout stages, he missed out. Kieran Read played consistently well for the All Blacks, and Toby Faletau did well for Wales, but the best No. 8 overall was Imanol Harinordoquy. Despite some disappointing

performances from France up to the final, he was never less than top-class and he deserves to be selected.

From so many really good flank forwards, the final pairing came down to the two captains who gave everything in the final – the All Blacks' Richie McCaw at open-side and Thierry Dusautoir of France at blind-side. The pick of the challengers is led by David Pocock of Australia, All Black Jerome Kaino and Sam Warburton of Wales.

The choice of lock forwards was fairly straightforward. Victor Matfield was the star of the South African pack once again, and for the second World Cup in succession he makes the World XV. Alongside Matfield, Lionel Nallet is chosen ahead of James Horwill of Australia and All Black Brad Thorn. Nallet was a tower of strength to France throughout the tournament and had an immense game in the final. Both Matfield and Nallet are number five jumpers, but both are versatile enough to play together in the same team.

At loose-head prop, Tony Woodcock of New Zealand just edged out Rodrigo Roncero of Argentina, and at tight-head, Nicolas Mas of France was a clear-cut selection. The choice of hooker was very difficult. The candidates were William Servat of France, Mario Ledesma of Argentina, Bismarck du Plessis of South Africa, Stephen Moore of Australia and Keven Mealamu of New Zealand. William Servat was the choice.

The captain of this team has to be Richie McCaw.

Italy's classy No. 8 and captain, Sergio Parisse, about to score his country's first try in the Pool C match against the USA.

RUGBY WORLD CUP 2011: WORLD XV

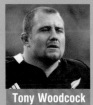
Tony Woodcock
1

William Servat
2

Nicolas Mas
3

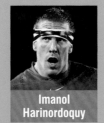
Lionel Nallet
4

Victor Matfield
5

Thierry Dusautoir
6

Imanol Harinordoquy
8

Richie McCaw
7

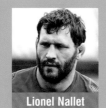
Mike Phillips
9

Felipe Contepomi
10

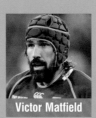
Ma'a Nonu
12

Jamie Roberts
13

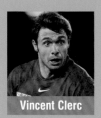
Vincent Clerc
11

Israel Dagg
15

George North
14

"That degree won't get you anywhere."

Conservative uncle

33° N – Zanskar, India

Live life without boundaries

When your children finish school, they won't be short of well-meant advice. But whether you encourage them to trust their instincts or your experience, you'll want to be able to support their education financially. Speak to HSBC Premier about creating a plan for your children's education.

HSBC Premier is subject to financial eligibility criteria and is available in over 40 countries and territories.

www.hsbcpremier.com

HSBC Premier

HSBC

The world's local bank

HIGHS AND LOWS
THANK YOU, NEW ZEALAND
CHRIS JONES

The biggest high at the 2011 Rugby World Cup was felt by the whole country when the All Blacks finally ended 24 years of hurt and defeated gallant France.

The 8-7 New Zealand victory at Eden Park set off the biggest mass drinking session the country had ever witnessed. The sound of police, ambulance and fire-engine sirens echoed around the streets of Auckland in the hours that followed the victory as fans from around the rugby world turned the centre into one big pub.

It may not have been a final of dramatic highs, but it was a fitting climax to a tournament that had far too many lows (mostly created by England players) but still rose to the occasion thanks to the warmth and generosity of the people – many of whom became unpaid helpers for the World Cup.

The All Blacks confirmed southern hemisphere domination of the sport, but at least Wales restored faith in the ability of northern hemisphere countries to play exciting rugby. However, they were reduced to 14 men in the semi-final with France when captain Sam Warburton, a young man of real poise and character, was sent off for a tip tackle when

everyone wanted the card to be coloured yellow. It disfigured the match and ensured Shane Williams, one of rugby's real magicians, who proves you don't have to be a giant to be great, would never play in a World Cup final and have at least one shot at a winner's medal. The genuine outpouring of feeling for Warburton was amazing, coming from both friend and foe, but the letter of the law was followed.

Besides the Warburton red card, this was a tournament shaped by injury. The loss of Dan Carter, the player whose image dominated Auckland from massive billboards showing the world's top points scorer in his boxers, was a blow that struck at the very heart of RWC 2011. Forget about the guy's magical playing skills, it was his personality, good humour and air of class that was so badly missed, particularly when England and France became such a long story of misguided actions and trash talking.

New Zealand, thanks to the emergence of Aaron Cruden, a young man who had recovered from testicular cancer, who wore Carter's No. 10 jersey in the final, had every reason to smile, and the feel-good factor was emphasised by everything scrum half Piri Weepu, a reformed character if

Piri Weepu leads the haka ahead of the quarter-final between the All Blacks and Argentina at Eden Park.

there ever was one, brought to the party. He lost his grandfather in the middle of the tournament, dragged two players out of a bar where they should not have been and generally became the focal point for a nation struggling to come to terms with the loss of Carter.

Weepu led the haka with a fierce pride never matched, and while many could claim this particular weapon in the All Blacks armoury has become too much like Hollywood, you do believe that the scrum half meant every word he uttered and felt each facial and body movement that is such a part of what is being offered. Given the way New Zealand dealt with the loss of Carter and his back-up Colin Slade, you really do wonder what on earth England and France were doing.

Their problems were all self-inflicted, not the result of bad luck. They were the two very public low points of the tournament, with England putting together a list of at least eight incidents that made them look boorish, unhelpful, ungrateful and frankly unwelcome guests in some parts of New Zealand. From Mike Tindall's appearance on a CCTV film with a blonde, to Manu Tuilagi's decision to jump off a perfectly sound ferry and swim across the busy Auckland harbour just because some equally idiotic members of the squad challenged him, to the lewd comments three other players made to a hotel worker, and the ball-tampering that implicated Jonny Wilkinson although it was two back-room men who did the time – this was England rugby at a very low ebb. What a dreadfully sad way for Wilkinson, the hero eight years previously, to end his cup career.

While other teams looked aghast at the negative publicity England were attracting, the French were doing their best to challenge Martin Johnson's men for the title of unhappiest squad at the tournament. The French problems stemmed from coach Marc Lièvremont, who did get his men to the final, but at what cost? He is now the ex-coach of France and everyone knew this was his fate before a ball had been kicked in anger. It was a ridiculous idea and one that only sowed the seeds of disquiet within a squad that didn't like Lièvremont's game plan and knew that the other coaches couldn't really help the players because power lay with one man.

Then there were the public admonishments from Lièvremont when players annoyed him, the painful attempts at retraction and the aftermath that usually involved Dimitri Yachvili, the gifted scrum half, trying to rally the troops and make the best of the latest mess created by his boss.

▬▬ **Christchurch, unable to stage its World Cup matches because of earthquake damage, welcomes the All Blacks and the Webb Ellis Cup. Atop the vehicle are coach Graham Henry, assistant coach Steve Hansen and Dan Carter.**

Unlike England, France did have a player who impressed in every match (although Manu Tuilagi tried his best) – full back Maxime Médard, whose attacking prowess was a welcome high amid the many French lows. And he also won, by a country mile, the contest to be the player who looked most like Wolverine from the X-Men films!

So with two of the senior unions of the sport behaving so badly, where could we turn for a beam of light to brighten the dark periods? Fittingly it came from the country whose flag boasts a picture of a blazing sun, and how we loved the Argentine fans! They travelled for 13 hours crammed into economy seats to be in New Zealand, many using the tournament to check out flights, hotels and bars for when they make regular trips to play New Zealand as the latest country to join the Tri-Nations tournament, making it now the Four Nations.

The Pumas fans were a gloriously bonkers bunch, bouncing their way around the South Island and then transferring their infectious love of the sport to Eden Park, where the blue-and-white wigs, blue-and-white costumes and national rugby jerseys created a little bit of the manic support that top football clubs in that South American country enjoy. The sight was hilarious of an exasperated press bench trying to watch the match from their position just behind a group of 30 Pumas fans as the sea of blue and white kept jumping up and down while singing. Of course, it wasn't that funny for the journos involved, but there wasn't a hint of trouble and the constant smiles said it all.

New Zealand did all of the Tier Two countries proud, with the smaller venues adopting the likes of Russia, USA, Romania, Georgia, Namibia and Japan. The costumes were fantastic, and who could ever forget the sight of a man and a woman wearing bikinis in USA colours while torrents of rain fell on them? Of course the low was the dreadfully unbalanced playing schedule that had those Tier Two nations on their knees before the last two rounds of matches; that will, thankfully, be addressed by the 2015 tournament.

You didn't need to ask the locals to adopt Tonga, Samoa and Fiji because so many tens of thousands of Islanders live in New Zealand, which meant Eden Park was full for the biggest of the matches between the sides: Fiji v Samoa. Flags were everywhere, along with heartfelt messages to family and friends back in the Islands, and what a joyous occasion it was, even if the match never really got off the ground.

To see Islands people go completely bonkers, you had to be present when Tonga defeated France, and that was one of the few real jaw-dropping results of the competition. Ireland's win over Australia was a shock because it upset what was supposed to be the draw that would produce a Wallabies v All Blacks final. The thousands of Irish fans, another reason to smile at the cup, painted everywhere green, and also came up with the best name for one of the hundreds of camper vans that criss-crossed the country. It was called 'Donncha O'Caravan', in honour of Irish lock Donncha O'Callaghan. Priceless.

This was the cup where the All Blacks played in a Stadium of Four Million, and that wasn't media hype, it was the truth. If only England and France could have realised what damage they were doing to their own reputations by tarnishing a World Cup played in a mate's backyard with the kind permission of the parents.

But those two badly behaved guests could not truly affect the image of the tournament, one that raised the spirits and showed New Zealand in the best possible light. The hosts did us all proud. Now, how many years will it take before they get round to taking down those huge billboards of Carter in his boxers?

■ **Argentina fans celebrate their 13-12 Pool B win over Scotland at Wellington Regional Stadium. The 'Puma' in front is reportedly Argentina flanker Genaro Fessia.**

STATISTICS

■ Rugby World Cup 1987-2011

Highest scores:
145	New Zealand v Japan (Bloemfontein, 1995)
142	Australia v Namibia (Adelaide, 2003)
111	England v Uruguay (Brisbane, 2003)

Biggest winning margin:
142	Australia v Namibia (Adelaide, 2003)
128	New Zealand v Japan (Bloemfontein, 1995)
98	England v Uruguay (Brisbane, 2003)
98	New Zealand v Italy (Huddersfield, 1999)

Most points by a player in a match:
45	Simon Culhane (New Zealand v Japan, 1995)
44	Gavin Hastings (Scotland v Ivory Coast, 1995)
42	Mat Rogers (Australia v Namibia, 2003)

Most tries by a player in a match:
6	Marc Ellis (New Zealand v Japan, 1995)
5	Chris Latham (Australia v Namibia, 2003)
5	Josh Lewsey (England v Uruguay, 2003)

Most points in one tournament:
126	Grant Fox (New Zealand, 1987)
113	Jonny Wilkinson (England, 2003)
112	Thierry Lacroix (France, 1995)

Leading aggregate World Cup scorers:
277	Jonny Wilkinson (England, 1999, 2003, 2007, 2011)
227	Gavin Hastings (Scotland, 1987, 1991, 1995)
195	Michael Lynagh (Australia, 1987, 1991, 1995)

Most tries in World Cups:
15	Jonah Lomu (New Zealand, 1995, 1999)
13	Doug Howlett (New Zealand, 2003, 2007)
11	Vincent Clerc (France, 2007, 2011)
	Chris Latham (Australia 1999, 2003, 2007)
	Joe Rokocoko (New Zealand 2003, 2007)
	Rory Underwood (England 1987, 1991, 1995)

Most tries in one tournament:
8	Jonah Lomu (New Zealand, 1999)
	Bryan Habana (South Africa, 2007)
7	Marc Ellis (New Zealand, 1995)
	Jonah Lomu (New Zealand, 1995)
	Doug Howlett (New Zealand, 2003)
	Mils Muliaina (New Zealand, 2003)
	Drew Mitchell (Australia, 2007)

Most tries in a match by a team:
22	Australia v Namibia (Adelaide, 2003)
21	New Zealand v Japan (Bloemfontein, 1995)

Most penalty goals in World Cups:
58	Jonny Wilkinson (England, 1999, 2003, 2007, 2011)
36	Gavin Hastings (Scotland, 1987, 1991, 1995)
35	Gonzalo Quesada (Argentina, 1999, 2003)

Most penalty goals in one tournament:
31	Gonzalo Quesada (Argentina, 1999)
26	Thierry Lacroix (France, 1995)
23	Jonny Wilkinson (England, 2003)

Most conversions in World Cups:
39	Gavin Hastings (Scotland, 1987, 1991, 1995)
37	Grant Fox (New Zealand, 1987, 1991)
36	Michael Lynagh (Australia, 1987, 1991, 1995)

Most conversions in one tournament:
30	Grant Fox (New Zealand, 1987)
22	Percy Montgomery (Soputh Africa, 2007)
20	Michael Lynagh (Australia, 1987)
	Simon Culhane (New Zealand, 1995)
	Leon MacDonald (New Zealand, 2003)
	Nick Evans (New Zealand, 2007)

Most dropped goals in World Cups:
14	Jonny Wilkinson (England, 1999, 2003, 2007, 2011)
6	Jannie de Beer (South Africa, 1999)
5	Rob Andrew (England, 1987, 1991, 1995)
	Gareth Rees (Canada, 1987, 1991, 1995, 1999)

Most dropped goals in one tournament:
8	Jonny Wilkinson (England, 2003)
6	Jannie de Beer (South Africa, 1999)
	Gregor Townsend (Scotland, 1999)

■ Rugby World Cup 2011

Leading point scorers

Player	Team	Points	Tries	Cons	Pens	DGs
Morné Steyn	South Africa	62	2	14	7	1
James O'Connor	Australia	52	1	13	7	0
Kurt Morath	Tonga	45	0	6	11	0
Ronan O'Gara	Ireland	44	0	10	8	0
Piri Weepu	New Zealand	41	0	4	11	0
Dimitri Yachvili	France	39	0	6	9	0
Morgan Parra	France	37	1	4	8	0
Colin Slade	New Zealand	36	1	14	1	0
James Arlidge	Japan	34	2	3	6	0
Vincent Clerc	France	30	6	0	0	0
Chris Ashton	England	30	6	0	0	0
Rhys Priestland	Wales	29	0	10	3	0
Merab Kvirikashvili	Georgia	28	0	2	8	0
Stephen Jones	Wales	28	0	11	2	0
Jonny Wilkinson	England	28	0	5	5	1
Felipe Contepomi	Argentina	26	1	3	5	0
Berrick Barnes	Australia	26	3	4	0	1
Tusi Pisi	Samoa	25	0	2	6	1
Keith Earls	Ireland	25	5	0	0	0
Israel Dagg	New Zealand	25	5	0	0	0
Adam Ashley-Cooper	Australia	25	5	0	0	0
Theuns Kotze	Namibia	24	1	2	2	3
Dan Parks	Scotland	24	0	0	5	3
Chris Paterson	Scotland	23	0	1	7	0
James Hook	Wales	23	0	1	7	0
Ander Monro	Canada	22	1	1	3	2
Seremaia Bai	Fiji	22	0	5	4	0
Jonathan Sexton	Ireland	21	0	3	4	1
Frans Steyn	South Africa	21	3	0	2	0
Toby Flood	England	21	0	9	1	0
Dan Carter	New Zealand	21	0	6	2	1
Paul Williams	Samoa	21	1	5	2	0
Sonny Bill Williams	New Zealand	20	4	0	0	0
Richard Kahui	New Zealand	20	4	0	0	0
Scott Williams	Wales	20	4	0	0	0
Zac Guildford	New Zealand	20	4	0	0	0
Mark Cueto	England	20	4	0	0	0
James Pritchard	Canada	20	0	4	4	0
Jerome Kaino	New Zealand	20	4	0	0	0
Vereniki Goneva	Fiji	20	4	0	0	0

Most tries

Player	Team	Tries
Vincent Clerc	France	6
Chris Ashton	England	6
Israel Dagg	New Zealand	5
Keith Earls	Ireland	5
Adam Ashley-Cooper	Australia	5
Mark Cueto	England	4
Jerome Kaino	New Zealand	4
Veroniki Goneva	Fiji	4
Scott Williams	Wales	4
Zac Guildford	New Zealand	4
Sonny Bill Williams	New Zealand	4
Richard Kahui	New Zealand	4

Most conversions

Player	Team	Conversions
Colin Slade	New Zealand	14
Morné Steyn	South Africa	14
James O'Connor	Australia	13
Stephen Jones	Wales	11
Rhys Priestland	Wales	10
Ronan O'Gara	Ireland	10
Toby Flood	England	9
Dimitri Yachvili	France	6
Ruan Pienaar	South Africa	6
Kurt Morath	Tonga	6

Most penalty goals

Player	Team	Penalties
Kurt Morath	Tonga	11
Piri Weepu	New Zealand	11
Dimitri Yachvili	France	9
Merab Kvirikashvili	Georgia	8
Ronan O'Gara	Ireland	8
Morgan Parra	France	8
James Hook	Wales	7
James O'Connor	Australia	7
Chris Paterson	Scotland	7
Morné Steyn	South Africa	7
James Arlidge	Japan	6
Tusi Pisi	Samoa	6
Mirco Bergamasco	Italy	5
Felipe Contepomi	Argentina	5
Danut Dumbrava	Romania	5
Dan Parks	Scotland	5
Jonny Wilkinson	England	5

Most dropped goals

Player	Team	Dropped goals
Theuns Kotze	Namibia	3
Dan Parks	Scotland	3
François Trinh-Duc	France	2
Ander Monro	Canada	2

Tries by country

New Zealand	40	Canada	9
Wales	29	Japan	8
Australia	28	Russia	8
South Africa	21	Fiji	7
England	20	Tonga	7
Ireland	16	Namibia	5
France	16	USA	4
Italy	13	Scotland	4
Argentina	11	Romania	3
Samoa	10	Georgia	3

9/9/2011 Auckland

New Zealand 41   Tonga 10

Tries: Dagg (2), Kahui (2), Kaino, Nonu
Cons: Carter (3), Slade
Pen: Carter

Try: Taumalolo
Con: Morath
Pen: Morath

15 Israel Dagg	15 Vunga Lilo
14 Richard Kahui	14 Viliame Iongi
13 Ma'a Nonu	13 Suka Hufanga
12 Sonny Bill Williams	12 Andrew Ma'ilei
11 Isaia Toeava	11 Siale Piutau
10 Dan Carter	10 Kurt Morath
9 Jimmy Cowan	9 Taniela Moa
1 Tony Woodcock	1 Soane Tonga'uiha
2 Andrew Hore	2 Aleki Lutui
3 Owen Franks	3 Taufa'ao Filise
4 Brad Thorn	4 Paino Hehea
5 Ali Williams	5 Joe Tuineau
6 Jerome Kaino	6 Sione Kalamafoni
7 Richie McCaw (c)	7 Finau Maka (c)
8 Victor Vito	8 Viliami Ma'afu
16 Corey Flynn*	16 Ephraim Taukafa*
17 Ben Franks*	17 Kisi Pulu*
18 Anthony Boric*	18 Sione Timani*
19 Sam Whitelock*	19 Sione Kalamafoni*
20 Piri Weepu*	20 Samiu Vahafolau*
21 Colin Slade*	21 Samisoni Fisilau*
22 Cory Jane*	22 Alipate Fatafehi*

Referee George Clancy

10/9/2011 Auckland

France 47   Japan 21

Tries: Pierre, Trinh-Duc, Clerc, Nallet, Papé, Parra
Cons: Yachvili (4)
Pens: Yachvili (3)

Tries: Arlidge (2)
Con: Arlidge
Pens: Arlidge (3)

15 Cédric Heymans	15 Shaun Webb
14 Vincent Clerc	14 Kosuke Endo
13 Aurélien Rougerie	13 Koji Taira
12 Fabrice Estebanez	12 Ryan Nicholas
11 Maxime Médard	11 Hirotoki Onozawa
10 François Trinh-Duc	10 James Arlidge
9 Dimitri Yachvili	9 Fumiaki Tanaka
1 Fabien Barcella	1 Hisateru Hirashima
2 William Servat	2 Shota Horie
3 Nicolas Mas	3 Kensuke Hatakeyama
4 Julien Pierre	4 Luke Thompson
5 Lionel Nallet	5 Toshizumi Kitagawa
6 Thierry Dusautoir (c)	6 Takashi Kikutani (c)
7 Imanol Harinordoquy	7 Michael Leitch
8 Raphaël Lakafia	8 Ryukoliniasi Holani
16 Dimitri Szarzewski*	16 Yusuke Aoki
17 Jean-Baptiste Poux*	17 Nozomu Fujita*
18 Pascal Papé*	18 Hitoshi Ono*
19 Julien Bonnaire*	19 Itaru Taniguchi*
20 Morgan Parra*	20 Atsushi Hiwasa*
21 David Skrela*	21 Murray Williams*
22 David Marty*	22 Alisi Tupuailai*

Referee Steve Walsh

14/9/2011 Whangarei

Tonga 20   Canada 25

Tries: Piutau (2)
Cons: Morath (2)
Pens: Morath (2)

Tries: Sinclair, Carpenter, Mackenzie
Cons: Pritchard (2)
Pens: Pritchard (2)

15 Kurt Morath	15 James Pritchard
14 Fetu'u Vainikolo	14 Ciaran Hearn
13 Siale Piutau	13 DTH van der Merwe
12 Alipate Fatafehi	12 Ryan Smith
11 William Helu	11 Phil Mackenzie
10 Taniela Moa	10 Ander Monro
9 Tomasi Palu	9 Ed Fairhurst
1 Sona Taumalolo	1 Hubert Buydens
2 Ephraim Takafuta	2 Pat Riordan (c)
3 Kisi Pulu	3 Jason Marshall
4 Sione Timani	4 Jebb Sinclair
5 Tukulua Lokotui	5 Jamie Cudmore
6 Finau Maka (c)	6 Adam Kleeberger
7 Sione Vaiomo'unga	7 Chauncey O'Toole
8 Samiu Vahafolau	8 Aaron Carpenter
16 Ilaisa Ma'asi*	16 Ryan Hamilton*
17 Soane Tonga'uiha*	17 Scott Franklin*
18 Halani Aulika*	18 Tyler Hotson*
19 Viliami Ma'afu*	19 Nanyak Dala*
20 Sione Kalamafoni*	20 Conor Trainor*
21 Viliame Iongi*	21 Sean White*
22 Alaska Taufa*	22 Nathan Hirayama*

Referee Jonathan Kaplan

16/9/2011 Hamilton

New Zealand 83   Japan 7

Tries: Smith, Kahui (2), Kaino, Mealamu, Ellis, Slade, SB Williams (2), Toeava, Hore, Nonu, Thomson
Cons: Slade (9)

Try: Onozawa
Con: Williams

15 Isaia Toeava	15 Taihei Ueda
14 Cory Jane	14 Takeshisa Usuzuki
13 Conrad Smith	13 Koji Taira
12 Ma'a Nonu	12 Yuta Imamura
11 Richard Kahui	11 Hirotoki Onozawa
10 Colin Slade	10 Murray Williams
9 Andy Ellis	9 Atsushi Hiwasa
1 Tony Woodcock	1 Naoki Kawamata
2 Keven Mealamu (c)	2 Yusuke Aoki
3 Owen Franks	3 Nozomu Fujita
4 Brad Thorn	4 Hitoshi Ono
5 Sam Whitelock	5 Toshizumi Kitagawa
6 Jerome Kaino	6 Itaru Taniguchi
7 Adam Thomson	7 Michael Leitch
8 Victor Vito	8 Takashi Kikutani (c)
16 Andrew Hore*	16 Hiroki Yuhara*
17 John Afoa*	17 Kensuke Hatakeyama*
18 Ali Williams*	18 Yuji Kitagawa*
19 Anthony Boric*	19 Sione Vatuvei*
20 Jimmy Cowan*	20 Tomoki Yoshida*
21 Piri Weepu*	21 Shaun Webb*
22 Sonny Bill Williams*	22 Alisi Tupuailai*

Referee Nigel Owens

18/9/2011 Napier

France 46   Canada 19

Tries: Clerc (3), Traille
Cons: Parra (4)
Pens: Parra (5)
DG: Trinh-Duc

Try: Smith
Con: Pritchard
Pens: Pritchard (2)
DGs: Monro (2)

15 Damien Traille	15 James Pritchard
14 Vincent Clerc	14 Ciaran Hearn
13 David Marty	13 DTH van der Merwe
12 Maxime Mermoz	12 Ryan Smith
11 Aurélien Rougerie	11 Phil Mackenzie
10 François Trinh-Duc	10 Ander Monro
9 Morgan Parra	9 Ed Fairhurst
1 Jean-Baptiste Poux	1 Hubert Buydens
2 William Servat	2 Pat Riordan (c)
3 Luc Ducalcon	3 Jason Marshall
4 Pascal Papé	4 Jebb Sinclair
5 Romain Millo-Chluski	5 Jamie Cudmore
6 Fulgence Ouedraogo	6 Adam Kleeberger
7 Julien Bonnaire	7 Chauncey O'Toole
8 Louis Picamoles	8 Aaron Carpenter
16 Guilhem Guirado*	16 Ryan Hamilton*
17 Fabien Barcella*	17 Scott Franklin*
18 Julien Pierre*	18 Tyler Hotson*
19 Imanol Harinordoquy*	19 Nanyak Dala*
20 Dimitri Yachvili*	20 Sean White*
21 Fabrice Estebanez	21 Nathan Hirayama*
22 Maxime Médard*	22 Conor Trainor*

Referee Craig Joubert

21/9/2011 Whangarei

Tonga 31   Japan 18

Tries: Ma'afu, Lokotui, Vainikolo
Cons: Morath (2)
Pens: Morath (4)

Tries: Hatakeyama, Leitch, Tupuailai
Pen: Webb

15 Vunga Lilo	15 Shaun Webb
14 Fetu'u Vainikolo	14 Kosuke Endo
13 Siale Piutau	13 Alisi Tupuailai
12 Alipate Fatafehi	12 Ryan Nicholas
11 Suka Hufanga	11 Hirotoki Onozawa
10 Kurt Morath	10 James Arlidge
9 Taniela Moa	9 Fumiaki Tanaka
1 Soane Tonga'uiha	1 Hisateru Hirashima
2 Aleki Lutui (c)	2 Shota Horie
3 Taufa'ao Filise	3 Kensuke Hatakeyama
4 Tukulua Lokotui	4 Luke Thompson
5 Paino Hehea	5 Toshizumi Kitagawa
6 Sione Kalamafoni	6 Itaru Taniguchi
7 Sione Vaiomo'unga	7 Michael Leitch
8 Viliami Ma'afu	8 Takashi Kikutani (c)
16 Ilaisa Ma'asi*	16 Yusuke Aoki
17 Sona Taumalolo*	17 Nozomu Fujita*
18 Halani Aulika*	18 Hitoshi Ono*
19 Joe Tuineau*	19 Sione Vatuvei*
20 Samiu Vahafolau*	20 Atsushi Hiwasa*
21 Samisoni Fisilau*	21 Takeshisa Usuzuki
22 Andrew Ma'ilei*	22 Murray Williams

Referee Dave Pearson

24/9/2011 Auckland

New Zealand 37   France 17

Tries: Thomson, Jane, Dagg (2), SB Williams
Cons: Carter (3)
Pen: Carter
DG: Carter

Tries: Mermoz, Trinh-Duc
Cons: Yachvili (2)
Pen: Yachvili

15 Israel Dagg	15 Damien Traille
14 Cory Jane	14 Vincent Clerc
13 Conrad Smith	13 Aurélien Rougerie
12 Ma'a Nonu	12 Maxime Mermoz
11 Richard Kahui	11 Maxime Médard
10 Dan Carter	10 Morgan Parra
9 Piri Weepu	9 Dimitri Yachvili
1 Tony Woodcock	1 Jean-Baptiste Poux
2 Keven Mealamu	2 Dimitri Szarzewski
3 Owen Franks	3 Luc Ducalcon
4 Brad Thorn	4 Pascal Papé
5 Sam Whitelock	5 Lionel Nallet
6 Jerome Kaino	6 Thierry Dusautoir (c)
7 Richie McCaw (c)	7 Julien Bonnaire
8 Adam Thomson	8 Louis Picamoles
16 Andrew Hore*	16 William Servat*
17 Ben Franks*	17 Fabien Barcella*
18 Ali Williams*	18 Julien Pierre*
19 Anthony Boric*	19 Imanol Harinordoquy*
20 Andy Ellis*	20 François Trinh-Duc*
21 Colin Slade*	21 Fabrice Estebanez*
22 Sonny Bill Williams*	22 Cédric Heymans*

Referee Alain Rolland

27/9/2011 Napier

Canada 23   Japan 23

Tries: van der Merwe, Mackenzie, Monro
Con: Pritchard
Pens: Monro (2)

Tries: Horie, Endo
Cons: Arlidge (2)
Pens: Arlidge (3)

15 James Pritchard	15 Shaun Webb
14 Matt Evans	14 Kosuke Endo
13 DTH van der Merwe	13 Alisi Tupuailai
12 Ryan Smith	12 Ryan Nicholas
11 Phil Mackenzie	11 Hirotoki Onozawa
10 Ander Monro	10 James Arlidge
9 Ed Fairhurst	9 Fumiaki Tanaka
1 Hubert Buydens	1 Hisateru Hirashima
2 Pat Riordan (c)	2 Shota Horie
3 Jason Marshall	3 Nozomu Fujita
4 Jebb Sinclair	4 Luke Thompson
5 Jamie Cudmore	5 Toshizumi Kitagawa
6 Adam Kleeberger	6 Sione Vatuvei
7 Chauncey O'Toole	7 Michael Leitch
8 Aaron Carpenter	8 Takashi Kikutani (c)
16 Ryan Hamilton*	16 Yusuke Aoki
17 Scott Franklin*	17 Kensuke Hatakeyama*
18 Tyler Hotson*	18 Hitoshi Ono*
19 Jeremy Kyne*	19 Toetu Taufa*
20 Sean White*	20 Atsushi Hiwasa*
21 Nathan Hirayama	21 Murray Williams*
22 Conor Trainor*	22 Bryce Robins*

Referee Jonathan Kaplan

1/10/2011 Wellington

France 14   Tonga 19

Try: Clerc
Pens: Yachvili (3)

Try: Hufanga
Con: Morath
Pens: Morath (4)

15 Maxime Médard	15 Vunga Lilo
14 Vincent Clerc	14 Viliame Iongi
13 Aurélien Rougerie	13 Siale Piutau
12 Maxime Mermoz	12 Andrew Ma'ilei
11 Alexis Palisson	11 Suka Hufanga
10 Morgan Parra	10 Kurt Morath
9 Dimitri Yachvili	9 Taniela Moa
1 Jean-Baptiste Poux	1 Soane Tonga'uiha
2 William Servat	2 Aleki Lutui
3 Luc Ducalcon	3 Kisi Pulu
4 Pascal Papé	4 Tukulua Lokotui
5 Lionel Nallet	5 Paino Hehea
6 Thierry Dusautoir (c)	6 Sione Kalamafoni
7 Julien Bonnaire	7 Finau Maka (c)
8 Raphaël Lakafia	8 Viliami Ma'afu
16 Dimitri Szarzewski	16 Ephraim Taukafa
17 Fabien Barcella*	17 Sona Taumalolo*
18 Julien Pierre*	18 Halani Aulika*
19 Imanol Harinordoquy*	19 Joe Tuineau*
20 François Trinh-Duc*	20 Samiu Vahafolau*
21 Fabrice Estebanez	21 Tomasi Palu*
22 Cédric Heymans*	22 Alipate Fatafehi*

Referee Steve Walsh

2/10/2011 Wellington

New Zealand 79   Canada 15

Tries: Guildford (4), Vito (2), Dagg, Muliaina, Cowan, Kaino (2), SB Williams
Cons: Slade (4), Weepu (4)
Pen: Slade

Tries: Trainor (2)
Con: Monro
Pen: Monro

15 Mils Muliaina	15 Matt Evans
14 Israel Dagg	14 Conor Trainor
13 Conrad Smith	13 DTH van der Merwe
12 Sonny Bill Williams	12 Ryan Smith
11 Zac Guildford	11 Phil Mackenzie
10 Colin Slade	10 Ander Monro
9 Jimmy Cowan	9 Ed Fairhurst
1 Tony Woodcock	1 Hubert Buydens
2 Andrew Hore (c)	2 Pat Riordan (c)
3 Owen Franks	3 Jason Marshall
4 Sam Whitelock	4 Jebb Sinclair
5 Ali Williams	5 Jamie Cudmore
6 Jerome Kaino	6 Adam Kleeberger
7 Victor Vito	7 Chauncey O'Toole
8 Kieran Read	8 Aaron Carpenter
16 Keven Mealamu*	16 Ryan Hamilton*
17 Ben Franks*	17 Scott Franklin*
18 Brad Thorn*	18 Andrew Tiedemann*
19 Anthony Boric*	19 Tyler Hotson*
20 Andy Ellis*	20 Nanyak Dala*
21 Piri Weepu*	21 Sean White*
22 Isaia Toeava*	22 Nathan Hirayama*

Referee Romain Poite

	P	W	D	L	F	A	BP	PTS
New Zealand	4	4	0	0	240	49	4	20
France	4	2	0	2	124	96	3	11
Tonga	4	2	0	2	80	98	1	9
Canada	4	1	1	2	82	168	0	6
Japan	4	0	1	3	69	184	0	2

* = used as substitute, including blood replacement

10/9/2011 Invercargill

Scotland 34
Tries: Blair, Ansbro, Danielli (2)
Con: Paterson
Pens: Paterson (4)

Romania 24
Tries: Lazar, Carpo
Con: Dimofte
Pens: Dumbrava (2), Dimofte (2)

15 Chris Paterson	15 Iulian Dumitras
14 Max Evans	14 Stefan Ciuntu
13 Joe Ansbro	13 Csaba Gal
12 Sean Lamont	12 Ionut Dimofte
11 Simon Danielli	11 Madalin Lemnaru
10 Ruaridh Jackson	10 Danut Dumbrava
9 Mike Blair	9 Lucian Sirbu
1 Allan Jacobsen	1 Mihaita Lazar
2 Ross Ford	2 Marius Tincu (c)
3 Geoff Cross	3 Paulica Ion
4 Richie Gray	4 Valentin Ursache
5 Alastair Kellock (c)	5 Cristian Petre
6 Kelly Brown	6 Mihai Macovei
7 John Barclay	7 Ovidiu Tonita
8 Richie Vernon	8 Daniel Carpo
16 Scott Lawson*	16 Bogdan Zebega*
17 Alasdair Dickinson*	17 Silviu Florea*
18 Nathan Hines*	18 Valentin Popirlan*
19 Ross Rennie*	19 Stelian Burcea*
20 Chris Cusiter*	20 Florin Surugiu*
21 Dan Parks*	21 Ionel Cazan*
22 Rory Lamont*	22 Florin Vlaicu*

Referee Dave Pearson

10/9/2011 Dunedin

Argentina 9
Pens: Contepomi, Rodriguez (2)

England 13
Try: Youngs
Con: Wilkinson
Pens: Wilkinson (2)

15 Martin Rodriguez	15 Ben Foden
14 Gonzalo Camacho	14 Chris Ashton
13 Gonzalo Tiesi	13 Manu Tuilagi
12 Santiago Fernández	12 Mike Tindall (c)
11 Horacio Agulla	11 Delon Armitage
10 Felipe Contepomi (c)	10 Jonny Wilkinson
9 Nicolás Vergallo	9 Richard Wigglesworth
1 Rodrigo Roncero	1 Andrew Sheridan
2 Mario Ledesma	2 Steve Thompson
3 Juan Figallo	3 Dan Cole
4 Manuel Carizza	4 Louis Deacon
5 Patricio Albacete	5 Courtney Lawes
6 Julio Farias Cabello	6 Tom Croft
7 J M Leguizamón	7 James Haskell
8 J M Fernández Lobbe	8 Nick Easter
16 Agustin Creevy*	16 Dylan Hartley*
17 Martin Scelzo*	17 Matt Stevens*
18 Mariano Galarza*	18 Tom Palmer*
19 Alejandro Campos*	19 Tom Wood*
20 Alfredo Lalanne*	20 Ben Youngs*
21 Marcelo Bosch*	21 Toby Flood*
22 Juan Imhoff*	22 Matt Banahan*

Referee Bryce Lawrence

14/9/2011 Invercargill

Scotland 15
Pens: Parks (4)
DG: Parks

Georgia 6
Pens: Kvirikashvili (2)

15 Rory Lamont	15 Revaz Gigauri
14 Max Evans	14 Irakli Machkhaneli
13 Nick De Luca	13 Davit Kacharava
12 Graeme Morrison	12 Tedore Zibzibadze
11 Sean Lamont	11 Alexander Todua
10 Dan Parks	10 Merab Kvirikashvili
9 Rory Lawson (c)	9 Irakli Abuseridze (c)
1 Allan Jacobsen	1 Davit Khinchagishvili
2 Ross Ford	2 Jaba Bregvadze
3 Euan Murray	3 Davit Zirakashvili
4 Nathan Hines	4 Levan Datunashvili
5 Jim Hamilton	5 Vakhtang Maisuradze
6 Alasdair Strokosch	6 Shalva Sutiashvili
7 Ross Rennie	7 Mamuka Gorgodze
8 Kelly Brown	8 Dimitri Basilaia
16 Dougie Hall	16 Akvsenti Giorgadze*
17 Geoff Cross	17 Davit Kubriashvili*
18 Alasdair Dickinson	18 Giorgi Chkhaidze*
19 Richie Gray*	19 Viktor Kolelishvili*
20 Richie Vernon	20 Bidzina Samkharadze*
21 Chris Cusiter	21 Lasha Khmaladze*
22 Chris Paterson	22 Malkhaz Urjukashvili*

Referee George Clancy

17/9/2011 Invercargill

Argentina 43
Tries: Fernández, Leguizamón, Figallo, Amorosino, Imhoff, Fessia
Cons: Rodriguez (5)
Pen: Rodriguez

Romania 8
Try: Cazan
Pen: Dimofte

15 L González Amorosino	15 Iulian Dumitras
14 Gonzalo Camacho	14 Madalin Lemnaru
13 Marcelo Bosch	13 Csaba Gal
12 Martin Rodriguez	12 Constantin Gheara
11 Horacio Agulla	11 Ionel Cazan
10 Santiago Fernández	10 Ionut Dimofte
9 Nicolás Vergallo	9 Florin Surugiu
1 Rodrigo Roncero	1 Mihaita Lazar
2 Mario Ledesma	2 Marius Tincu (c)
3 Juan Figallo	3 Paulica Ion
4 Manuel Carizza	4 Valentin Ursache
5 Patricio Albacete	5 Cristian Petre
6 Alejandro Campos	6 Mihai Macovei
7 J M Leguizamón	7 Ovidiu Tonita
8 J M Fernández Lobbe (c)	8 Daniel Carpo
16 Agustin Creevy*	16 Bogdan Zebega*
17 Martin Scelzo*	17 Silviu Florea*
18 Mariano Galarza*	18 Valentin Popirlan*
19 Genaro Fessia*	19 Daniel Ianus*
20 Alfredo Lalanne*	20 Valentin Calafeteanu*
21 Nicolás Sánchez*	21 Danut Dumbrava*
22 Juan Imhoff*	22 Florin Vlaicu*

Referee Steve Walsh

18/9/2011 Dunedin

England 41
Tries: Hape (2), Armitage, Tuilagi, Ashton (2)
Cons: Flood (4)
Pen: Flood

Georgia 10
Try: Basilaia
Con: Kvirikashvili
Pen: Kvirikashvili

15 Ben Foden	15 Revaz Gigauri
14 Chris Ashton	14 Irakli Machkhaneli
13 Manu Tuilagi	13 Davit Kacharava
12 Shontayne Hape	12 Tedore Zibzibadze
11 Delon Armitage	11 Alexander Todua
10 Toby Flood	10 Merab Kvirikashvili
9 Ben Youngs	9 Irakli Abuseridze (c)
1 Matt Stevens	1 Davit Khinchagishvili
2 Dylan Hartley	2 Jaba Bregvadze
3 Dan Cole	3 Davit Kubriashvili
4 Simon Shaw	4 Ilia Zedginidze
5 Tom Palmer	5 Vakhtang Maisuradze
6 Tom Wood	6 Shalva Sutiashvili
7 Lewis Moody (c)	7 Mamuka Gorgodze
8 James Haskell	8 Dimitri Basilaia
16 Steve Thompson*	16 Goderdzi Shvelidze*
17 Alex Corbisiero*	17 Davit Zirakashvili*
18 Tom Croft*	18 Levan Datunashvili*
19 Louis Deacon*	19 Giorgi Chkhaidze*
20 Joe Simpson*	20 Bidzina Samkharadze*
21 Jonny Wilkinson*	21 Givi Berishvili*
22 Matt Banahan*	22 Lasha Khmaladze*

Referee Jonathan Kaplan

24/9/2011 Dunedin

England 67
Tries: Cueto (3), Ashton (3), Youngs, Foden, Tuilagi, Croft
Cons: Wilkinson (3), Flood (4)
Pen: Wilkinson

Romania 3
Pen: Dumbrava

15 Ben Foden	15 Florin Vlaicu
14 Chris Ashton	14 Stefan Ciuntu
13 Manu Tuilagi	13 Ionel Cazan
12 Mike Tindall	12 Iulian Dumitras
11 Mark Cueto	11 Adrian Apostol
10 Jonny Wilkinson	10 Danut Dumbrava
9 Ben Youngs	9 Lucian Sirbu
1 Alex Corbisiero	1 Nicolae Nere
2 Steve Thompson	2 Bogdan Zebega
3 Dan Cole	3 Silviu Florea
4 Louis Deacon	4 Valentin Popirlan
5 Tom Palmer	5 Cristian Petre (c)
6 Tom Croft	6 Stelian Burcea
7 Lewis Moody (c)	7 Cosmin Ratiu
8 James Haskell	8 Ovidiu Tonita
16 Lee Mears*	16 Marius Tincu*
17 David Wilson*	17 Paulica Ion*
18 Simon Shaw*	18 Mihai Macovei*
19 Tom Wood*	19 Daniel Ianus*
20 Richard Wigglesworth*	20 Valentin Calafeteanu*
21 Toby Flood*	21 Csaba Gal*
22 Delon Armitage*	22 Catalin Nicolae*

Referee Romain Poite

25/9/2011 Wellington

Argentina 13
Try: Amorosino
Con: Contepomi
Pens: Contepomi (2)

Scotland 12
Pens: Paterson, Jackson
DGs: Jackson, Parks

15 Martin Rodriguez	15 Chris Paterson
14 Gonzalo Camacho	14 Max Evans
13 Marcelo Bosch	13 Nick De Luca
12 Felipe Contepomi (c)	12 Graeme Morrison
11 Horacio Agulla	11 Sean Lamont
10 Santiago Fernández	10 Ruaridh Jackson
9 Nicolás Vergallo	9 Rory Lawson (c)
1 Rodrigo Roncero	1 Allan Jacobsen
2 Mario Ledesma	2 Ross Ford
3 Juan Figallo	3 Geoff Cross
4 Manuel Carizza	4 Richie Gray
5 Patricio Albacete	5 Jim Hamilton
6 Julio Farias Cabello	6 Alasdair Strokosch
7 J M Leguizamón	7 John Barclay
8 J M Fernández Lobbe	8 Kelly Brown
16 Agustin Creevy*	16 Dougie Hall*
17 Martin Scelzo*	17 Alasdair Dickinson*
18 Mariano Galarza*	18 Nathan Hines*
19 Genaro Fessia*	19 Richie Vernon*
20 Alfredo Lalanne*	20 Mike Blair*
21 L González Amorosino*	21 Dan Parks*
22 Juan Imhoff*	22 Simon Danielli*

Referee Wayne Barnes

28/9/2011 Palmerston North

Georgia 25
Try: Gorgodze
Con: Kvirikashvili
Pens: Kvirikashvili (5), Urjukashvili

Romania 9
Pens: Dumbrava (2), Vlaicu

15 Lasha Khmaladze	15 Iulian Dumitras
14 Revaz Gigauri	14 Stefan Ciuntu
13 Davit Kacharava	13 Csaba Gal
12 Tedore Zibzibadze	12 Ionut Dimofte
11 Alexander Todua	11 Madalin Lemnaru
10 Merab Kvirikashvili	10 Danut Dumbrava
9 Irakli Abuseridze (c)	9 Florin Surugiu
1 Davit Khinchagishvili	1 Mihaita Lazar
2 Jaba Bregvadze	2 Marius Tincu (c)
3 Davit Zirakashvili	3 Paulica Ion
4 Ilia Zedginidze	4 Valentin Ursache
5 Vakhtang Maisuradze	5 Cristian Petre
6 Giorgi Chkhaidze	6 Mihai Macovei
7 Mamuka Gorgodze	7 Ovidiu Tonita
8 Dimitri Basilaia	8 Daniel Carpo
16 Goderdzi Shvelidze	16 Bogdan Zebega
17 Vasil Kakovin*	17 Silviu Florea*
18 Levan Datunashvili*	18 Valentin Popirlan*
19 Givi Berishvili*	19 Daniel Ianus*
20 Bidzina Samkharadze*	20 Valentin Calafeteanu*
21 Irakli Chkhikvadze*	21 Constantin Gheara*
22 Malkhaz Urjukashvili*	22 Florin Vlaicu*

Referee Dave Pearson

1/10/2011 Auckland

England 16
Try: Ashton
Con: Flood
Pens: Wilkinson (2)
DG: Wilkinson

Scotland 12
Pens: Paterson (2), Parks
DG: Parks

15 Ben Foden	15 Chris Paterson
14 Chris Ashton	14 Max Evans
13 Manu Tuilagi	13 Joe Ansbro
12 Mike Tindall	12 Sean Lamont
11 Delon Armitage	11 Simon Danielli
10 Jonny Wilkinson	10 Ruaridh Jackson
9 Ben Youngs	9 Mike Blair
1 Matt Stevens	1 Allan Jacobsen
2 Steve Thompson	2 Ross Ford
3 Dan Cole	3 Euan Murray
4 Louis Deacon	4 Richie Gray
5 Courtney Lawes	5 Alastair Kellock (c)
6 Tom Croft	6 Alasdair Strokosch
7 Lewis Moody (c)	7 John Barclay
8 James Haskell	8 Richie Vernon
16 Dylan Hartley*	16 Scott Lawson
17 Alex Corbisiero*	17 Alasdair Dickinson*
18 Tom Palmer*	18 Nathan Hines*
19 Nick Easter*	19 Ross Rennie*
20 Richard Wigglesworth*	20 Chris Cusiter*
21 Toby Flood*	21 Dan Parks*
22 Matt Banahan*	22 Nick De Luca*

Referee Craig Joubert

2/10/2011 Palmerston North

Argentina 25
Tries: Imhoff, Contepomi, Gosio
Cons: Contepomi, Bosch
Pens: Contepomi (2)

Georgia 7
Try: Khmaladze
Con: Urjukashvili

15 L González Amorosino	15 Malkhaz Urjukashvili
14 Horacio Agulla	14 Lekso Gugava
13 Marcelo Bosch	13 Davit Kacharava
12 Felipe Contepomi (c)	12 Tedore Zibzibadze
11 Juan Imhoff	11 Alexander Todua
10 Santiago Fernández	10 Lasha Khmaladze
9 Nicolás Vergallo	9 Irakli Abuseridze (c)
1 Marcos Ayerza	1 Vasil Kakovin
2 Mario Ledesma	2 Akvsenti Giorgadze
3 Juan Figallo	3 Davit Kubriashvili
4 Mariano Galarza	4 Levan Datunashvili
5 Patricio Albacete	5 Vakhtang Maisuradze
6 Julio Farias Cabello	6 Giorgi Chkhaidze
7 J M Leguizamón	7 Viktor Kolelishvili
8 Leonardo Senatore	8 Mamuka Gorgodze
16 Agustin Creevy*	16 Jaba Bregvadze*
17 Martin Scelzo*	17 Goderdzi Shvelidze*
18 Tomás Vallejos Cinalli*	18 Ilia Zedginidze*
19 Genaro Fessia*	19 Giorgi Nemsadze*
20 Alfredo Lalanne*	20 Giorgi Chkhaidze*
21 Agustin Gosio*	21 Merab Kvirikashvili*
22 Martin Rodriguez*	22 Lasha Malaguradze*

Referee Alain Rolland

FINAL POOL B

	P	W	D	L	F	A	BP	PTS
England	4	4	0	0	137	34	2	18
Argentina	4	3	0	1	90	40	2	14
Scotland	4	2	0	2	73	59	3	11
Georgia	4	1	0	3	48	90	0	4
Romania	4	0	0	4	44	169	0	0

11/9/2011 Auckland

Australia 32
Tries: Alexander, Ashley-Cooper, O'Connor, Ioane
Cons: O'Connor (3)
Pens: Cooper (2)

Italy 6
Pens: Bergamasco (2)

Australia	Italy
15 Kurtley Beale	15 Andrea Masi
14 Adam Ashley-Cooper	14 Tommaso Benvenuti
13 Anthony Faingaa	13 Gonzalo Canale
12 Pat McCabe	12 Gonzalo Garcia
11 Digby Ioane	11 Mirco Bergamasco
10 Quade Cooper	10 Luciano Orquera
9 Will Genia	9 Fabio Semenzato
1 Sekope Kepu	1 Andrea Lo Cicero
2 Stephen Moore	2 Leonardo Ghiraldini
3 Ben Alexander	3 Martin Castrogiovanni
4 Dan Vickerman	4 Carlo Antonio Del Fava
5 James Horwill (c)	5 Cornelius Van Zyl
6 Rocky Elsom	6 Alessandro Zanni
7 David Pocock	7 Robert Julian Barbieri
8 Radike Samo	8 Sergio Parisse (c)
16 Tatafu Polota-Nau*	16 Tommaso D'Apice
17 James Slipper*	17 Lorenzo Cittadini*
18 Rob Simmons*	18 Marco Bortolami*
19 Ben McCalman*	19 Paul Derbyshire*
20 Scott Higginbotham*	20 Edoardo Gori*
21 Luke Burgess*	21 Riccardo Bocchino*
22 James O'Connor*	22 Luke McLean*

Referee Alain Rolland

11/9/2011 New Plymouth

Ireland 22
Tries: Bowe (2), Best
Cons: Sexton, O'Gara
Pen: Sexton

USA 10
Try: Emerick
Con: Malifa
Pen: Paterson

Ireland	USA
15 Geordan Murphy	15 Blaine Scully
14 Tommy Bowe	14 Takudzwa Ngwenya
13 Brian O'Driscoll (c)	13 Paul Emerick
12 Gordon D'Arcy	12 Andrew Suniula
11 Keith Earls	11 James Paterson
10 Jonathan Sexton	10 Roland Suniula
9 Conor Murray	9 Mike Petri
1 Tom Court	1 Mike MacDonald
2 Rory Best	2 Phil Thiel
3 Mike Ross	3 Shawn Pittman
4 Donncha O'Callaghan	4 John van der Giessen
5 Paul O'Connell	5 Hayden Smith
6 Stephen Ferris	6 Louis Stanfill
7 Shane Jennings	7 Todd Clever (c)
8 Jamie Heaslip	8 Nic Johnson
16 Jerry Flannery*	16 Chris Biller*
17 Tony Buckley*	17 Mate Moeakiola*
18 Donnacha Ryan	18 Scott LaValla
19 Denis Leamy*	19 Pat Danahy
20 Eoin Reddan*	20 Tim Usasz*
21 Ronan O'Gara*	21 Valenese Malifa*
22 Andrew Trimble*	22 Colin Hawley

Referee Craig Joubert

15/9/2011 New Plymouth

Russia 6
Pens: Kushnarev, Rachkov

USA 13
Try: Petri
Con: Wyles
Pens: Wyles (2)

Russia	USA
15 Igor Klyuchnikov	15 Chris Wyles
14 Vasily Artemyev	14 Takudzwa Ngwenya
13 Konstantin Rachkov	13 Paul Emerick
12 Alexey Makovetskiy	12 Andrew Suniula
11 Vladimir Ostroushko	11 James Paterson
10 Yury Kushnarev	10 Roland Suniula
9 Alexander Shakirov	9 Mike Petri
1 Sergey Popov	1 Mike MacDonald
2 Vladislav Korshunov (c)	2 Chris Biller
3 Ivan Prishchepenko	3 Mate Moeakiola
4 Alexander Voytov	4 John van der Giessen
5 Denis Antonov	5 Hayden Smith
6 Artem Fatakhov	6 Louis Stanfill
7 Andrey Garbuzov	7 Todd Clever (c)
8 Viatcheslav Grachev	8 Nic Johnson
16 Valeriy Tsnobiladze	16 Phil Thiel
17 Vladimir Botvinnikov*	17 Shawn Pittman*
18 Alexander Khrokin	18 Scott LaValla*
19 Adam Byrnes*	19 Pat Danahy
20 Alexander Yanyushkin	20 Tim Usasz*
21 Victor Gresev*	21 Valenese Malifa
22 Andrey Kuzin	22 Blaine Scully*

Referee Dave Pearson

17/9/2011 Auckland

Australia 6
Pens: O'Connor (2)

Ireland 15
Pens: Sexton (2), O'Gara (2)
DG: Sexton

Australia	Ireland
15 Kurtley Beale	15 Rob Kearney
14 James O'Connor	14 Tommy Bowe
13 Anthony Faingaa	13 Brian O'Driscoll (c)
12 Pat McCabe	12 Gordon D'Arcy
11 Adam Ashley-Cooper	11 Keith Earls
10 Quade Cooper	10 Jonathan Sexton
9 Will Genia	9 Eoin Reddan
1 Sekope Kepu	1 Cian Healy
2 Tatafu Polota-Nau	2 Rory Best
3 Ben Alexander	3 Mike Ross
4 Dan Vickerman	4 Donncha O'Callaghan
5 James Horwill (c)	5 Paul O'Connell
6 Rocky Elsom	6 Stephen Ferris
7 Ben McCalman	7 Sean O'Brien
8 Radike Samo	8 Jamie Heaslip
16 Saia Faingaa	16 Sean Cronin
17 James Slipper*	17 Tom Court*
18 Rob Simmons*	18 Donnacha Ryan
19 Wycliff Palu*	19 Denis Leamy
20 Scott Higginbotham*	20 Conor Murray*
21 Luke Burgess	21 Ronan O'Gara*
22 Drew Mitchell*	22 Andrew Trimble*

Referee Bryce Lawrence

20/9/2011 Nelson

Italy 53
Tries: Parisse, Toniolatti (2), Benvenuti (2), Penalty try, Gori, McLean, Zanni
Cons: Bocchino (4)

Russia 17
Tries: Yanyushkin, Ostroushko, Makovetskiy
Con: Rachkov

Italy	Russia
15 Andrea Masi	15 Igor Klyuchnikov
14 Giulio Toniolatti	14 Vasily Artemyev
13 Tommaso Benvenuti	13 Andrey Kuzin
12 Matteo Pratichetti	12 Alexey Makovetskiy
11 Luke McLean	11 Vladimir Ostroushko
10 Riccardo Bocchino	10 Konstantin Rachkov
9 Edoardo Gori	9 Alexander Shakirov
1 Salvatore Perugini	1 Vladimir Botvinnikov
2 Fabio Ongaro	2 Vladislav Korshunov (c)
3 Lorenzo Cittadini	3 Ivan Prishchepenko
4 Quintin Geldenhuys	4 Alexander Voytov
5 Marco Bortolami	5 Adam Byrnes
6 Paul Derbyshire	6 Viatcheslav Grachev
7 Mauro Bergamasco	7 Andrey Garbuzov
8 Sergio Parisse (c)	8 Victor Gresev
16 Tommaso D'Apice*	16 Valeriy Tsnobiladze*
17 Martin Castrogiovanni*	17 Alexander Khrokin*
18 Cornelius Van Zyl*	18 Denis Antonov*
19 Alessandro Zanni*	19 Artem Fatakhov*
20 Pablo Canavosio*	20 Alexander Yanyushkin*
21 Gonzalo Canale*	21 Mikhail Sidorov*
22 Alberto Sgarbi*	22 Yury Kushnarev*

Referee Wayne Barnes

23/9/2011 Wellington

Australia 67
Tries: Horne, Elsom, Beale, Faingaa (2), Mitchell, McCabe, Ashley-Cooper (3), Samo
Cons: Cooper (2), Barnes (4)

USA 5
Try: Gagiano

Australia	USA
15 Kurtley Beale	15 Blaine Scully
14 Adam Ashley-Cooper	14 Colin Hawley
13 Anthony Faingaa	13 Tai Enosa
12 Rob Horne	12 Junior Sifa
11 Drew Mitchell	11 Kevin Swiryn
10 Quade Cooper	10 Valenese Malifa
9 Will Genia (c)	9 Tim Usasz (c)
1 James Slipper	1 Shawn Pittman
2 Tatafu Polota-Nau	2 Phil Thiel
3 Ben Alexander	3 Eric Fry
4 Rob Simmons	4 Scott LaValla
5 Nathan Sharpe	5 Hayden Smith
6 Rocky Elsom	6 Inaki Basauri
7 Ben McCalman	7 Pat Danahy
8 Wycliff Palu	8 JJ Gagiano
16 Stephen Moore*	16 Brian McClenahan*
17 Sekope Kepu*	17 Mate Moeakiola
18 Dan Vickerman*	18 Louis Stanfill*
19 Radike Samo*	19 Nic Johnson*
20 Luke Burgess*	20 Mike Petri*
21 Berrick Barnes*	21 Roland Suniula
22 Pat McCabe*	22 Chris Wyles*

Referee Nigel Owens

25/9/2011 Rotorua

Ireland 62
Tries: McFadden, O'Brien, Boss, Earls (2), Trimble, Kearney, Jennings, Buckley
Cons: O'Gara (6), Sexton
Pen: O'Gara

Russia 12
Tries: Artemyev, Simplikevich
Con: Rachkov

Ireland	Russia
15 Rob Kearney	15 Vasily Artemyev
14 Fergus McFadden	14 Denis Simplikevich
13 Keith Earls	13 Andrey Kuzin
12 Paddy Wallace	12 Sergey Trishin
11 Andrew Trimble	11 Vladimir Ostroushko
10 Ronan O'Gara	10 Konstantin Rachkov
9 Isaac Boss	9 Alexander Yanyushkin (c)
1 Cian Healy	1 Sergey Popov
2 Sean Cronin	2 Valeriy Tsnobiladze
3 Tony Buckley	3 Alexander Khrokin
4 Donncha O'Callaghan	4 Denis Antonov
5 Leo Cullen (c)	5 Adam Byrnes
6 Donnacha Ryan	6 Artem Fatakhov
7 Sean O'Brien	7 Andrey Garbuzov
8 Jamie Heaslip	8 Victor Gresev
16 Rory Best	16 Evgenii Matveev*
17 Mike Ross*	17 Ivan Prishchepenko*
18 Denis Leamy*	18 Alexey Travkin*
19 Shane Jennings*	19 Alexander Voytov*
20 Eoin Reddan*	20 Andrey Bykanov*
21 Jonathan Sexton*	21 Mikhail Sidorov*
22 Geordan Murphy*	22 Mikhail Babaev*

Referee Craig Joubert

27/9/2011 Nelson

Italy 27
Tries: Parisse, Orquera, Castrogiovanni, Penalty try
Cons: Mi Bergamasco (2)
Pen: Mi Bergamasco

USA 10
Try: Wyles
Con: Wyles
Pen: Wyles

Italy	USA
15 Luke McLean	15 Chris Wyles
14 Tommaso Benvenuti	14 Takudzwa Ngwenya
13 Gonzalo Canale	13 Paul Emerick
12 Gonzalo Garcia	12 Andrew Suniula
11 Mirco Bergamasco	11 James Paterson
10 Luciano Orquera	10 Roland Suniula
9 Fabio Semenzato	9 Mike Petri
1 Salvatore Perugini	1 Mike MacDonald
2 Leonardo Ghiraldini	2 Chris Biller
3 Martin Castrogiovanni	3 Mate Moeakiola
4 Quintin Geldenhuys	4 John van der Giessen
5 Cornelius Van Zyl	5 Hayden Smith
6 Alessandro Zanni	6 Louis Stanfill
7 Mauro Bergamasco	7 Todd Clever (c)
8 Sergio Parisse (c)	8 Nic Johnson
16 Fabio Ongaro*	16 Phil Thiel*
17 Andrea Lo Cicero*	17 Shawn Pittman*
18 Marco Bortolami	18 Scott LaValla*
19 Paul Derbyshire*	19 Pat Danahy
20 Edoardo Gori*	20 Tim Usasz*
21 Riccardo Bocchino*	21 Valenese Malifa*
22 Giulio Toniolatti*	22 Blaine Scully*

Referee George Clancy

1/10/2011 Nelson

Australia 68
Tries: Barnes (2), Mitchell (2), McCalman, Pocock (2), Moore, Ashley-Cooper, Ma'afu
Cons: O'Connor (9)

Russia 22
Tries: Ostroushko, Simplikevich, Rachkov
Cons: Rachkov (2)
DG: Rachkov

Australia	Russia
15 James O'Connor	15 Vasily Artemyev
14 Radike Samo	14 Denis Simplikevich
13 Adam Ashley-Cooper	13 Andrey Kuzin
12 Berrick Barnes	12 Alexey Makovetskiy
11 Drew Mitchell	11 Vladimir Ostroushko
10 Quade Cooper	10 Yury Kushnarev
9 Luke Burgess	9 Alexander Yanyushkin
1 James Slipper	1 Sergey Popov
2 Stephen Moore	2 Vladislav Korshunov (c)
3 Sekope Kepu	3 Ivan Prishchepenko
4 James Horwill (c)	4 Alexander Voytov
5 Nathan Sharpe	5 Adam Byrnes
6 Scott Higginbotham	6 Artem Fatakhov
7 David Pocock	7 Viatcheslav Grachev
8 Ben McCalman	8 Victor Gresev
16 Tatafu Polota-Nau	16 Evgenii Matveev*
17 Saia Faingaa*	17 Vladimir Botvinnikov*
18 Salesi Ma'afu*	18 Alexey Travkin*
19 Rob Simmons*	19 Andrey Garbuzov*
20 Rocky Elsom*	20 Alexander Shakirov*
21 Will Genia	21 Konstantin Rachkov*
22 Nick Phipps*	22 Mikhail Babaev*

Referee Bryce Lawrence

2/10/2011 Dunedin

Ireland 36
Tries: O'Driscoll, Earls (2)
Cons: O'Gara (2), Sexton
Pens: O'Gara (4), Sexton

Italy 6
Pens: Mi Bergamasco (2)

Ireland	Italy
15 Rob Kearney	15 Andrea Masi
14 Tommy Bowe	14 Tommaso Benvenuti
13 Brian O'Driscoll (c)	13 Gonzalo Canale
12 Gordon D'Arcy	12 Gonzalo Garcia
11 Keith Earls	11 Mirco Bergamasco
10 Ronan O'Gara	10 Luciano Orquera
9 Conor Murray	9 Fabio Semenzato
1 Cian Healy	1 Salvatore Perugini
2 Rory Best	2 Leonardo Ghiraldini
3 Mike Ross	3 Martin Castrogiovanni
4 Donncha O'Callaghan	4 Quintin Geldenhuys
5 Paul O'Connell	5 Cornelius Van Zyl
6 Stephen Ferris	6 Alessandro Zanni
7 Sean O'Brien	7 Mauro Bergamasco
8 Jamie Heaslip	8 Sergio Parisse (c)
16 Sean Cronin*	16 Fabio Ongaro*
17 Tom Court*	17 Andrea Lo Cicero*
18 Donnacha Ryan*	18 Marco Bortolami*
19 Denis Leamy*	19 Paul Derbyshire*
20 Eoin Reddan*	20 Edoardo Gori*
21 Jonathan Sexton*	21 Riccardo Bocchino*
22 Andrew Trimble*	22 Luke McLean*

Referee Jonathan Kaplan

FINAL POOL C

	P	W	D	L	F	A	BP	PTS
Ireland	4	4	0	0	135	34	1	17
Australia	4	3	0	1	173	48	3	15
Italy	4	2	0	2	92	95	2	10
USA	4	1	0	3	38	122	0	4
Russia	4	0	0	4	57	196	1	1

10/9/2011 Rotorua

Fiji 49
Tries: Goneva (4), Nakarawa, Nalaga
Cons: Bai (5)
Pens: Bai (3)

Namibia 25
Tries: Koll, Botha
Pens: Kotze (2)
DGs: Kotze (3)

15 Kini Murimurivalu	15 Chrysander Botha
14 Vereniki Goneva	14 Danie Dames
13 Gabiriele Lovobalavu	13 Danie van Wyk
12 Seremaia Bai	12 Piet van Zyl
11 Napolioni Nalaga	11 Conrad Marais
10 Waisea Luveniyali	10 Theuns Kotze
9 Nemia Kenatale Ranuku	9 Eugene Jantjies
1 Campese Ma'afu	1 Johannes Redelinghuys
2 Viliame Veikoso	2 Hugo Horn
3 Deacon Manu (c)	3 Raoul Larson
4 Leone Nakarawa	4 Heinz Koll
5 Wame Lewaravu	5 Nico Esterhuyse
6 Dominiko Waqaniburotu	6 Tinus du Plessis
7 Malakai Ravulo	7 Jacques Burger (c)
8 Netani Talei	8 Jacques Nieuwenhuis
16 Sunia Koto*	16 Egbertus O'Callaghan*
17 Waisea Daveta*	17 Jané du Toit*
18 Sekonaia Kalou*	18 Pieter-Jan van Lill*
19 Akapusi Qera*	19 Rohan Kitshoff*
20 Vitori Buatava*	20 Ryan de la Harpe*
21 Albert Vulivuli*	21 Darryl de la Harpe*
22 Iliesa Keresoni*	22 Llewellyn Winkler*

Referee Nigel Owens

11/9/2011 Wellington

South Africa 17
Tries: F Steyn, Hougaard
Cons: M Steyn (2)
Pen: M Steyn

Wales 16
Try: Faletau
Con: Hook
Pens: Hook (3)

15 Frans Steyn	15 James Hook
14 JP Pietersen	14 George North
13 Jaque Fourie	13 Jonathan Davies
12 Jean de Villiers	12 Jamie Roberts
11 Bryan Habana	11 Shane Williams
10 Morné Steyn	10 Rhys Priestland
9 Fourie du Preez	9 Mike Phillips
1 Tendai Mtawarira	1 Paul James
2 John Smit (c)	2 Huw Bennett
3 Jannie du Plessis	3 Adam Jones
4 Victor Matfield	4 Luke Charteris
5 Danie Rossouw	5 Alun-Wyn Jones
6 Heinrich Brüssow	6 Dan Lydiate
7 Schalk Burger	7 Sam Warburton (c)
8 Pierre Spies	8 Toby Faletau
16 Bismarck du Plessis*	16 Lloyd Burns*
17 Gurthrö Steenkamp*	17 Ryan Bevington*
18 CJ van der Linde*	18 Bradley Davies*
19 Johann Muller*	19 Andy Powell*
20 Willem Alberts*	20 Tavis Knoyle*
21 Francois Hougaard*	21 Scott Williams*
22 Butch James*	22 Leigh Halfpenny*

Referee Wayne Barnes

14/9/2011 Rotorua

Samoa 49
Tries: Fotuali'i, Tuilagi (3), Williams, Penalty try
Cons: T. Pisi (2), Williams (3)
Pens: T. Pisi (2), Williams

Namibia 12
Tries: van Wyk, Kotze
Con: Kotze

15 Paul Williams	15 Chrysander Botha
14 Sailosi Tagicakibau	14 Danie Dames
13 George Pisi	13 Danie van Wyk
12 Seilala Mapusua	12 Piet van Zyl
11 Alesana Tuilagi	11 Llewellyn Winkler
10 Tusi Pisi	10 Theuns Kotze
9 Kahn Fotuali'i	9 Eugene Jantjies
1 Sakaria Taulafo	1 Johannes Redelinghuys
2 Mahonri Schwalger (c)	2 Hugo Horn
3 Anthony Perenise	3 Raoul Larson
4 Daniel Leo	4 Heinz Koll
5 Kane Thompson	5 Hendrik Franken
6 Taiasina Tuifua	6 Rohan Kitshoff
7 Maurie Fa'asavalu	7 Jacques Burger (c)
8 George Stowers	8 Pieter-Jan van Lill
16 Ti'i Paulo*	16 Egbertus O'Callaghan*
17 Census Johnston*	17 Jané du Toit*
18 Joe Tekori*	18 Nico Esterhuyse*
19 Ofisa Treviranus*	19 Renaud van Neel*
20 Junior Poluleuiligaga*	20 Ryan de la Harpe*
21 Eliota Fuimaono-Sapolu*	21 Darryl de la Harpe*
22 Tasesa Lavea*	22 Tertius Losper*

Referee Romain Poite

17/9/2011 Wellington

South Africa 49
Tries: Steenkamp, Fourie, F Steyn, M Steyn, Mtawarira, Rossouw
Cons: M Steyn (5)
Pens: F Steyn, M Steyn (2)

Fiji 3
Pen: Bai

15 Pat Lambie	15 Kini Murimurivalu
14 Odwa Ndungane	14 Vereniki Goneva
13 Jaque Fourie	13 Gabiriele Lovobalavu
12 Frans Steyn	12 Seremaia Bai
11 JP Pietersen	11 Napolioni Nalaga
10 Morné Steyn	10 Waisea Luveniyali
9 Fourie du Preez	9 Nemia Kenatale Ranuku
1 Gurthrö Steenkamp	1 Campese Ma'afu
2 John Smit (c)	2 Sunia Koto
3 Jannie du Plessis	3 Deacon Manu (c)
4 Bakkies Botha	4 Leone Nakarawa
5 Danie Rossouw	5 Wame Lewaravu
6 Heinrich Brüssow	6 Dominiko Waqaniburotu
7 Schalk Burger	7 Akapusi Qera
8 Pierre Spies	8 Sakiusa Matadigo
16 Bismarck du Plessis*	16 Talemaitoga Tuapati*
17 Tendai Mtawarira*	17 Waisea Daveta*
18 Francois Louw*	18 Netani Talei*
19 Willem Alberts*	19 Sisa Koyamaibole*
20 Francois Hougaard*	20 Vitori Buatava*
21 Ruan Pienaar*	21 Nicky Little*
22 Juan de Jongh*	22 Ravai Fatiaki*

Referee Romain Poite

18/9/2011 Hamilton

Wales 17
Try: Shane Williams
Pens: Hook (2), Priestland (2)

Samoa 10
Try: Perenise
Con: Williams
Pen: Williams

15 James Hook	15 Paul Williams
14 George North	14 Sailosi Tagicakibau
13 Jonathan Davies	13 George Pisi
12 Jamie Roberts	12 Seilala Mapusua
11 Shane Williams	11 Alesana Tuilagi
10 Rhys Priestland	10 Tasesa Lavea
9 Mike Phillips	9 Kahn Fotuali'i
1 Paul James	1 Sakaria Taulafo
2 Huw Bennett	2 Mahonri Schwalger (c)
3 Adam Jones	3 Anthony Perenise
4 Luke Charteris	4 Daniel Leo
5 Alun-Wyn Jones	5 Kane Thompson
6 Dan Lydiate	6 Ofisa Treviranus
7 Sam Warburton (c)	7 Maurie Fa'asavalu
8 Toby Faletau	8 George Stowers
16 Lloyd Burns*	16 Ti'i Paulo*
17 Gethin Jenkins*	17 Census Johnston*
18 Bradley Davies*	18 Joe Tekori*
19 Andy Powell*	19 Manaia Salavea*
20 Tavis Knoyle*	20 Jeremy Su'a*
21 Scott Williams*	21 Eliota Fuimaono-Sapolu*
22 Leigh Halfpenny*	22 James So'oialo*

Referee Alain Rolland

22/9/2011 Auckland

South Africa 87
Tries: Aplon (2), Habana, Penalty try, Fourie, F Steyn, M Steyn, de Jongh (2), Hougaard (2), Rossouw
Cons: M Steyn (6), Pienaar (6)
Pen: M Steyn

Namibia 0

15 Pat Lambie	15 Chrysander Botha
14 Gio Aplon	14 Danie Dames
13 Jaque Fourie	13 Danie van Wyk
12 Frans Steyn	12 Piet van Zyl
11 Bryan Habana	11 Heini Bock
10 Morné Steyn	10 Theuns Kotze
9 Francois Hougaard	9 Eugene Jantjies
1 Gurthrö Steenkamp	1 Johannes Redelinghuys
2 John Smit (c)	2 Egbertus O'Callaghan
3 CJ van der Linde	3 Marius Visser
4 Bakkies Botha	4 Heinz Koll
5 Danie Rossouw	5 Nico Esterhuyse
6 Willem Alberts	6 Tinus du Plessis
7 Schalk Burger	7 Jacques Burger (c)
8 Pierre Spies	8 Jacques Nieuwenhuis
16 Chilliboy Ralepelle*	16 Hugo Horn*
17 Tendai Mtawarira*	17 Jané du Toit*
18 Francois Louw*	18 Pieter-Jan van Lill*
19 Heinrich Brüssow*	19 Rohan Kitshoff*
20 Fourie du Preez*	20 Ryan de la Harpe*
21 Ruan Pienaar*	21 Darryl de la Harpe*
22 Juan de Jongh*	22 Conrad Marais*

Referee George Clancy

25/9/2011 Auckland

Fiji 7
Try: Talei
Con: Luveniyali

Samoa 27
Tries: Fotuali'i, Stowers
Con: Williams
Pens: Pisi (4)
DG: Pisi

15 Kini Murimurivalu	15 Paul Williams
14 Vereniki Goneva	14 Sailosi Tagicakibau
13 Gabiriele Lovobalavu	13 George Pisi
12 Seremaia Bai	12 Seilala Mapusua
11 Napolioni Nalaga	11 Alesana Tuilagi
10 Nicky Little	10 Tusi Pisi
9 Nemia Kenatale Ranuku	9 Kahn Fotuali'i
1 Campese Ma'afu	1 Sakaria Taulafo
2 Sunia Koto	2 Mahonri Schwalger (c)
3 Deacon Manu (c)	3 Census Johnston
4 Sekonaia Kalou	4 Daniel Leo
5 Leone Nakarawa	5 Kane Thompson
6 Netani Talei	6 Taiasina Tuifua
7 Malakai Ravulo	7 Maurie Fa'asavalu
8 Sisa Koyamaibole	8 George Stowers
16 Talemaitoga Tuapati*	16 Ti'i Paulo*
17 Setefano Somoca*	17 Anthony Perenise*
18 Rupeni Nasiga*	18 Filipo Levi*
19 Akapusi Qera*	19 Manaia Salavea*
20 Vitori Buatava*	20 Jeremy Su'a*
21 Albert Vulivuli*	21 Eliota Fuimaono-Sapolu*
22 Waisea Luveniyali*	22 James So'oialo*

Referee Bryce Lawrence

26/9/2011 New Plymouth

Wales 81
Tries: S Williams (3), Brew, Faletau, Jenkins, North (2), J Davies, L Williams, Byrne, A-W Jones
Cons: S Jones (6), Priestland (3)
Pen: S Jones

Namibia 7
Try: Koll
Con: Kotze

15 Lee Byrne	15 Chrysander Botha
14 Leigh Halfpenny	14 Danie van Wyk
13 Jonathan Davies	13 Piet van Zyl
12 Scott Williams	12 Darryl de la Harpe
11 Aled Brew	11 Danie Dames
10 Stephen Jones	10 Theuns Kotze
9 Tavis Knoyle	9 Eugene Jantjies
1 Gethin Jenkins	1 Johannes Redelinghuys
2 Lloyd Burns	2 Hugo Horn
3 Craig Mitchell	3 Jané du Toit
4 Bradley Davies	4 Heinz Koll
5 Alun-Wyn Jones	5 Nico Esterhuyse
6 Ryan Jones	6 Tinus du Plessis
7 Sam Warburton (c)	7 Jacques Burger (c)
8 Toby Faletau	8 Jacques Nieuwenhuis
16 Ken Owens*	16 Egbertus O'Callaghan*
17 Ryan Bevington*	17 Raoul Larson*
18 Luke Charteris*	18 Uakazuwaka Kazombiaze*
19 Andy Powell*	19 Rohan Kitshoff*
20 Lloyd Williams*	20 Ryan de la Harpe*
21 Rhys Priestland*	21 Tertius Losper*
22 George North*	22 David Philander*

Referee Steve Walsh

30/9/2011 Auckland

South Africa 13
Try: Habana
Con: M Steyn
Pens: F Steyn, M Steyn

Samoa 5
Try: Stowers

15 Pat Lambie	15 Paul Williams
14 JP Pietersen	14 David Lemi
13 Jaque Fourie	13 Seilala Mapusua
12 Frans Steyn	12 Eliota Fuimaono-Sapolu
11 Bryan Habana	11 Alesana Tuilagi
10 Morné Steyn	10 Tusi Pisi
9 Fourie du Preez	9 Kahn Fotuali'i
1 Tendai Mtawarira	1 Sakaria Taulafo
2 Bismarck du Plessis	2 Mahonri Schwalger (c)
3 Jannie du Plessis	3 Census Johnston
4 Danie Rossouw	4 Daniel Leo
5 Victor Matfield (c)	5 Kane Thompson
6 Heinrich Brüssow	6 Taiasina Tuifua
7 Schalk Burger	7 Maurie Fa'asavalu
8 Pierre Spies	8 George Stowers
16 John Smit*	16 Ole Avei*
17 Gurthrö Steenkamp*	17 Anthony Perenise*
18 CJ van der Linde*	18 Logovi'i Mulipola*
19 Willem Alberts*	19 Joe Tekori*
20 Francois Louw*	20 Ofisa Treviranus*
21 Francois Hougaard*	21 Junior Poluleuiligaga*
22 Jean de Villiers*	22 George Pisi*

Referee Nigel Owens

2/10/2011 Hamilton

Wales 66
Tries: Roberts (2), S Williams, North, Warburton, Burns, Halfpenny, L Williams, J Davies
Cons: Priestland (5), S Jones (4)
Pen: Priestland

Fiji 0

15 Lee Byrne	15 Iliesa Keresoni
14 Leigh Halfpenny	14 Albert Vulivuli
13 Scott Williams	13 Ravai Fatiaki
12 Jamie Roberts	12 Gabiriele Lovobalavu
11 George North	11 Michael Tagicakibau
10 Rhys Priestland	10 Nicky Little
9 Mike Phillips	9 Vitori Buatava
1 Gethin Jenkins	1 Waisea Daveta
2 Huw Bennett	2 Sunia Koto
3 Adam Jones	3 Setefano Somoca
4 Bradley Davies	4 Leone Nakarawa
5 Luke Charteris	5 Wame Lewaravu
6 Ryan Jones	6 Rupeni Nasiga
7 Sam Warburton (c)	7 Sakiusa Matadigo
8 Toby Faletau	8 Netani Talei (c)
16 Lloyd Burns*	16 Viliame Veikoso*
17 Paul James*	17 Campese Ma'afu*
18 Alun-Wyn Jones*	18 Malakai Ravulo*
19 Andy Powell*	19 Akapusi Qera*
20 Lloyd Williams*	20 Nemia Kenatale Ranuku*
21 Stephen Jones*	21 Seremaia Bai*
22 Jonathan Davies*	22 Vereniki Goneva*

Referee Wayne Barnes

FINAL POOL D

	P	W	D	L	F	A	BP	PTS
South Africa	4	4	0	0	166	24	2	18
Wales	4	3	0	1	180	34	3	15
Samoa	4	2	0	2	91	49	2	10
Fiji	4	1	0	3	59	167	1	5
Namibia	4	0	0	4	44	266	0	0

8/10/2011 Wellington

Ireland 10
Try: Earls
Con: O'Gara
Pen: O'Gara

Wales 22
Tries: Shane Williams, Phillips, J Davies
Cons: Priestland (2)
Pen: Halfpenny

15 Rob Kearney	15 Leigh Halfpenny
14 Tommy Bowe	14 George North
13 Brian O'Driscoll (c)	13 Jonathan Davies
12 Gordon D'Arcy	12 Jamie Roberts
11 Keith Earls	11 Shane Williams
10 Ronan O'Gara	10 Rhys Priestland
9 Conor Murray	9 Mike Phillips
1 Cian Healy	1 Gethin Jenkins
2 Rory Best	2 Huw Bennett
3 Mike Ross	3 Adam Jones
4 Donncha O'Callaghan	4 Luke Charteris
5 Paul O'Connell	5 Alun-Wyn Jones
6 Stephen Ferris	6 Dan Lydiate
7 Sean O'Brien	7 Sam Warburton (c)
8 Jamie Heaslip	8 Toby Faletau
16 Sean Cronin	16 Lloyd Burns
17 Tom Court	17 Paul James
18 Donnacha Ryan*	18 Bradley Davies*
19 Denis Leamy*	19 Ryan Jones
20 Eoin Reddan*	20 Lloyd Williams
21 Jonathan Sexton*	21 James Hook*
22 Andrew Trimble*	22 Scott Williams

Referee Craig Joubert

8/10/2011 Auckland

England 12
Tries: Foden, Cueto
Con: Wilkinson

France 19
Tries: Clerc, Médard
Pens: Yachvili (2)
DG: Trinh-Duc

15 Ben Foden	15 Maxime Médard
14 Chris Ashton	14 Vincent Clerc
13 Manu Tuilagi	13 Aurélien Rougerie
12 Toby Flood	12 Maxime Mermoz
11 Mark Cueto	11 Alexis Palisson
10 Jonny Wilkinson	10 Morgan Parra
9 Ben Youngs	9 Dimitri Yachvili
1 Matt Stevens	1 Jean-Baptiste Poux
2 Steve Thompson	2 William Servat
3 Dan Cole	3 Nicolas Mas
4 Louis Deacon	4 Pascal Papé
5 Tom Palmer	5 Lionel Nallet
6 Tom Croft	6 Thierry Dusautoir (c)
7 Lewis Moody (c)	7 Julien Bonnaire
8 Nick Easter	8 Imanol Harinordoquy
16 Dylan Hartley*	16 Dimitri Szarzewski*
17 Alex Corbisiero*	17 Fabien Barcella*
18 Simon Shaw*	18 Julien Pierre*
19 Courtney Lawes*	19 Louis Picamoles*
20 James Haskell*	20 François Trinh-Duc*
21 Richard Wigglesworth*	21 David Marty*
22 Matt Banahan*	22 Cédric Heymans*

Referee Steve Walsh

15/10/2011 Auckland

Wales 8
Try: Phillips
Pen: Hook

France 9
Pens: Parra (3)

15 Leigh Halfpenny	15 Maxime Médard
14 George North	14 Vincent Clerc
13 Jonathan Davies	13 Aurélien Rougerie
12 Jamie Roberts	12 Maxime Mermoz
11 Shane Williams	11 Alexis Palisson
10 James Hook	10 Morgan Parra
9 Mike Phillips	9 Dimitri Yachvili
1 Gethin Jenkins	1 Jean-Baptiste Poux
2 Huw Bennett	2 William Servat
3 Adam Jones	3 Nicolas Mas
4 Luke Charteris	4 Pascal Papé
5 Alun-Wyn Jones	5 Lionel Nallet
6 Dan Lydiate	6 Thierry Dusautoir (c)
7 Sam Warburton (c)	7 Julien Bonnaire
8 Toby Faletau	8 Imanol Harinordoquy
16 Lloyd Burns	16 Dimitri Szarzewski*
17 Paul James*	17 Fabien Barcella*
18 Bradley Davies*	18 Julien Pierre*
19 Ryan Jones*	19 Fulgence Ouedraogo*
20 Lloyd Williams	20 François Trinh-Duc*
21 Stephen Jones*	21 Jean-Marc Doussain*
22 Scott Williams*	22 Cédric Heymans

Referee Alain Rolland

16/10/2011 Auckland

Australia 6
Pen: O'Connor
DG: Cooper

New Zealand 20
Try: Nonu
Pens: Weepu (4)
DG: Cruden

15 Adam Ashley-Cooper	15 Israel Dagg
14 James O'Connor	14 Cory Jane
13 Anthony Faingaa	13 Conrad Smith
12 Pat McCabe	12 Ma'a Nonu
11 Digby Ioane	11 Richard Kahui
10 Quade Cooper	10 Aaron Cruden
9 Will Genia	9 Piri Weepu
1 Sekope Kepu	1 Tony Woodcock
2 Stephen Moore	2 Keven Mealamu
3 Ben Alexander	3 Owen Franks
4 Dan Vickerman	4 Brad Thorn
5 James Horwill (c)	5 Sam Whitelock
6 Rocky Elsom	6 Jerome Kaino
7 David Pocock	7 Richie McCaw (c)
8 Radike Samo	8 Kieran Read
16 Tatafu Polota-Nau*	16 Andrew Hore*
17 James Slipper*	17 Ben Franks*
18 Rob Simmons*	18 Ali Williams*
19 Ben McCalman*	19 Victor Vito*
20 Luke Burgess	20 Andy Ellis*
21 Berrick Barnes*	21 Stephen Donald
22 Rob Horne*	22 Sonny Bill Williams*

Referee Craig Joubert

9/10/2011 Wellington

South Africa 9
Pens: Steyn (2)
DG: Steyn

Australia 11
Try: Horwill
Pens: O'Connor (2)

15 Pat Lambie	15 Kurtley Beale
14 JP Pietersen	14 James O'Connor
13 Jaque Fourie	13 Adam Ashley-Cooper
12 Jean de Villiers	12 Pat McCabe
11 Bryan Habana	11 Digby Ioane
10 Morné Steyn	10 Quade Cooper
9 Fourie du Preez	9 Will Genia
1 Gurthrö Steenkamp	1 Sekope Kepu
2 John Smit (c)	2 Stephen Moore
3 Jannie du Plessis	3 Ben Alexander
4 Danie Rossouw	4 Dan Vickerman
5 Victor Matfield	5 James Horwill (c)
6 Heinrich Brüssow	6 Rocky Elsom
7 Schalk Burger	7 David Pocock
8 Pierre Spies	8 Radike Samo
16 Bismarck du Plessis*	16 Tatafu Polota-Nau*
17 CJ van der Linde	17 James Slipper*
18 Willem Alberts*	18 Nathan Sharpe*
19 Francois Louw*	19 Ben McCalman*
20 Francois Hougaard*	20 Luke Burgess
21 Butch James	21 Berrick Barnes*
22 Gio Aplon	22 Anthony Faingaa*

Referee Bryce Lawrence

9/10/2011 Auckland

New Zealand 33
Tries: Read, Thorn
Con: Cruden
Pens: Weepu (7)

Argentina 10
Try: Cabello
Con: Contepomi
Pen: Bosch

15 Mils Muliaina	15 Martin Rodriguez
14 Cory Jane	14 Gonzalo Camacho
13 Conrad Smith	13 Marcelo Bosch
12 Ma'a Nonu	12 Felipe Contepomi (c)
11 Sonny Bill Williams	11 Horacio Agulla
10 Colin Slade	10 Santiago Fernández
9 Piri Weepu	9 Nicolás Vergallo
1 Tony Woodcock	1 Rodrigo Roncero
2 Keven Mealamu	2 Mario Ledesma
3 Owen Franks	3 Juan Figallo
4 Brad Thorn	4 Manuel Carizza
5 Sam Whitelock	5 Patricio Albacete
6 Jerome Kaino	6 Julio Farías Cabello
7 Richie McCaw (c)	7 J M Leguizamón
8 Kieran Read	8 Leonardo Senatore
16 Andrew Hore*	16 Agustín Creevy*
17 John Afoa*	17 Martín Scelzo*
18 Ali Williams*	18 Marcos Ayerza*
19 Victor Vito*	19 Alejandro Campos*
20 Jimmy Cowan*	20 Alfredo Lalanne*
21 Aaron Cruden*	21 L González Amorosino*
22 Isaia Toeava*	22 Juan Imhoff*

Referee Nigel Owens

21/10/2011 Eden Park, Auckland

WALES **AUSTRALIA**

Wales 18
Tries: Shane Williams, Halfpenny
Con: S Jones
Pens: Hook, S Jones

Australia 21
Tries: Barnes, McCalman
Con: O'Connor
Pens: O'Connor (2)
DG: Barnes

15 Leigh Halfpenny	15 Kurtley Beale
14 George North	14 James O'Connor
13 Jonathan Davies	13 Adam Ashley-Cooper
12 Jamie Roberts	12 Berrick Barnes
11 Shane Williams	11 Digby Ioane
10 James Hook	10 Quade Cooper
9 Mike Phillips	9 Will Genia
1 Gethin Jenkins (c)	1 James Slipper
2 Huw Bennett	2 Tatafu Polota-Nau
3 Paul James	3 Salesi Ma'afu
4 Luke Charteris	4 James Horwill (c)
5 Bradley Davies	5 Nathan Sharpe
6 Dan Lydiate	6 Scott Higginbotham
7 Toby Faletau	7 David Pocock
8 Ryan Jones	8 Ben McCalman
16 Lloyd Burns*	16 Saia Faingaa*
17 Ryan Bevington*	17 Ben Alexander*
18 Alun-Wyn Jones*	18 Rob Simmons*
19 Andy Powell*	19 Radike Samo*
20 Lloyd Williams*	20 Luke Burgess*
21 Stephen Jones*	21 Anthony Faingaa*
22 Scott Williams*	22 Rob Horne*

Referee Wayne Barnes

23/10/2011 Eden Park, Auckland

FRANCE **NEW ZEALAND**

France 7
Try: Dusautoir
Con: Trinh-Duc

New Zealand 8
Try: Woodcock
Pen: Donald

15 Maxime Médard	15 Israel Dagg
14 Vincent Clerc	14 Cory Jane
13 Aurélien Rougerie	13 Conrad Smith
12 Maxime Mermoz	12 Ma'a Nonu
11 Alexis Palisson	11 Richard Kahui
10 Morgan Parra	10 Aaron Cruden
9 Dimitri Yachvili	9 Piri Weepu
1 Jean-Baptiste Poux	1 Tony Woodcock
2 William Servat	2 Keven Mealamu
3 Nicolas Mas	3 Owen Franks
4 Pascal Papé	4 Brad Thorn
5 Lionel Nallet	5 Sam Whitelock
6 Thierry Dusautoir (c)	6 Jerome Kaino
7 Julien Bonnaire	7 Richie McCaw (c)
8 Imanol Harinordoquy	8 Kieran Read
16 Dimitri Szarzewski*	16 Andrew Hore*
17 Fabien Barcella*	17 Ben Franks
18 Julien Pierre*	18 Ali Williams*
19 Fulgence Ouedraogo	19 Adam Thomson
20 Jean-Marc Doussain*	20 Andy Ellis*
21 François Trinh-Duc*	21 Stephen Donald*
22 Damien Traille*	22 Sonny Bill Williams*

Referee Craig Joubert

* = used as substitute, including blood replacement